The Book *of* Virtues

By the same author

Treasure Chest for Public Speaking
Treasure Chest of virtue
Treasure Chest of Motivation

Little Red Books Series

Little Red Book of Slang-Chat room Slang
ittle Red Book of English Vocabulary Today
Little Red Book of Grammar Made Easy
Little Red Book of English Proverbs
Little Red Book of Prepositions
Little Red Book of Idioms and Phrases
Little Red Book of Euphemisms
Little Red Book of Effective Speaking Skills
Little Red Book of Writing Skills
Little Red Book of Verbal Phrases
Little Red Book of Nouns and Pronouns
Little Red Book of Synonyms
Little Red Book of Antonyms

A2Z Book Series

A2Z Quiz Book
A2Z Book of Origins
Treasure Chest of Classical Literature

Others

The Book of Fun Facts
The Book of More Fun Facts
Read Write Right: Common errors in English

Fiction

Vilayti Pani: The Anglo-Indian Novel

The Book *of* Virtues

Terry O'Brien

RUPA
PUBLICATIONS INDIA

Copyright © Terry O'Brien 2011

Published 2011 by
Rupa Publications India Pvt. Ltd.
7/16, Ansari Road, Daryaganj,
New Delhi 110 002

Sales Centres:
Allahabad Bengaluru Chennai
Hyderabad Jaipur Kathmandu
Kolkata Mumbai

All rights reserved.
No part of this publication may be reproduced, stored in a retrieval system, or transmitted, in any form or by any means, electronic, mechanical, photocopying, recording or otherwise, without the prior permission of the publishers.

The author asserts the moral right to be identified as the author of this work

Typeset by
Anvi Composers
19, A1-B, DDA Market
Paschim Vihar
New Delhi 110 063

Printed in India by
Shree Maitrey Printech Pvt. Ltd.
A-84, Sector-2
Noida-201301

I dedicate this book to late Prof. A. P. O'Brien, my father, friend, guide and mentor, who inspired me to the canon of excellence:
re-imagining what's essential

INTRODUCTION

The three questions that need to be answered throughout one's life:
- Who am I?
- Who ought I to become?
- How ought I to get there?

The three replies to the three questions is an on- going learning lesson. Some of the answers are found in poems and stories for all and sundry, be it fairy tales or real life events. The canvass of life has within it the footprints of time where one finds glimpses of virtues.

The Book of Virtues is an anthology of pieces that have helped me share values with my students and friends. It is not a treatise on doctrinaire; it is a book where one can read and ponder over and re-think the fact that life is a celebration.

Do remember: *This world is our exercise book on which we do our sums. We may, however, scribble on the pages and even tear the pages*!

Happy Reading!

Terry O'Brien

THE PRAYER

Saint Francis of Assisi

Lord, make me an instrument of your peace.
Where there is hatred, let me sow love.
Where there is injury, pardon.
Where there is doubt, faith.
Where there is despair, hope.
Where there is darkness, light.
Where there is sadness, joy.
O Divine Master,
Grant that I may not so much seek to be consoled, as to console;
To be understood, as to understand;
To be loved, as to love.
For it is in giving that we receive.
It is in pardoning that we are pardoned,
And it is in dying that we are born to Eternal Life.
    Amen.

Let Dogs Delight to Bark and Bite

The dogs delight to bark and bite,
For God hath made them so;
Let bears and lions growl and fight,
For 'tis their nature too.

**But, children, you should never let such
angry passions rise;
Your little hands were never made
To tear each other's eyes.**

Little Fred

In which we learn how to retire for the evening.

When little Fred was called to bed,
He always acted right;
He kissed Mama,
And then Papa,
And wished them all good night.
He made no noise, like naughty boys,
But gently up the stairs directly went, when he was sent,
And always said his prayers.

The Vulture

This one belongs on the refrigerator door.

The Vulture eats between his meals,
And that's the reason why
He very, very rarely feels
As well as you or I.
His eye is dull, his head is bald,
His neck is growing thinner.
**Oh, what a lesson for us all
To only eat at dinner.**

The Boy and the Nuts

Aesop

One good, practical reason for controlling our cravings is that if we grasp for too much, we may end up getting nothing at all.

    A little boy once found a jar of nuts on the table. "I would like some of these nuts," he thought. "I'm sure Mother would give them to me if she were here. I'll take a big handful." So he reached into the jar and grabbed as many as he could hold. But when he tried to pull his hand out, he found the neck of the jar was too small. His hand was held fast, but he did not want to drop any of the nuts. He tried again and again, but he couldn't get the whole handful out. At last he began to cry. Just then his mother came into the room. "What's the matter?" she asked. "I can't take this handful of nuts out of the jar," sobbed the boy. "Well, don't be so greedy," his mother replied. "Just take two or three, and you'll have no trouble getting your hand out." "How easy that was," said the boy as he left the table. "I might have thought of that myself."

The Goose That Laid the Golden Eggs

Aesop

Here is Aesop's classic fable about plenty not being enough, about what happens when "having it all" becomes the motto of the day.

    A man and his wife had the good fortune to possess a goose that laid a golden egg every day. Lucky though they were, they soon began to think they were not getting rich fast enough, and, imagining the bird must be made of gold inside, they decided to kill it in order to secure the whole store of precious metal at once. But when they cut it open they found it was just like any other goose. Thus, they neither got rich all at once, as they had hoped, nor enjoyed any longer the daily addition to their wealth. Much wants more and loses all.

The Fox and the Crow

Aesop

Vanity is largely a matter of self—control, or lack thereof. Others may try to feed our ego, but it is up to us to constrain it.

A coal—black crow once stole a piece of meat. She flew to a tree and held the meat in her beak. A fox, who saw her, wanted the meat for himself, so he looked up into the tree and said, "How beautiful you are, my friend! Your feathers are fairer than the dove's "Is your voice as sweet as your form is beautiful? If so, you must be the queen of birds." The crow was so happy in his praise that she opened her mouth to show how she could sing. Down fell the piece of meat. The fox seized upon it and ran away.

Boy Wanted

This "want ad" appeared in the early part of this century.

WANTED—

A boy that stands straight, sits straight, acts straight, and talks straight;

A boy whose fingernails are not in mourning, whose ears are clean, whose shoes are polished, whose clothes are brushed, whose hair is combed, and whose teeth are well cared for;

A boy who listens carefully when he is spoken to, who asks questions when he does not understand, and does not ask questions about things that are none of his business;

A boy that moves quickly and makes as little noise about it as possible;

A boy who whistles in the street, but does not whistle where he ought to keep still;

A boy who looks cheerful, has a ready smile for everybody, and never sulks;

A boy who is polite to every man and respectful to every woman and girl;

A boy who does not smoke cigarettes and has no desire to learn how;

A boy who is more eager to know how to speak good English than to talk slang;

A boy that never bullies other boys nor allows other boys to bully him;

A boy who, when he does not know a thing, says, "I don't know," and

when he has made a mistake says, "I'm sorry," and when he is asked to do a thing says, "I'll try";
A boy who looks you right in the eye and tells the truth every time;
A boy who is eager to read good books;
A boy who would rather put in his spare time at the gymnasium than to gamble in a back room;
A boy who does not want to be "smart" nor in any wise to attract attention;
A boy who would rather lose his job or be expelled from school than to tell a lie!; a cad;
A boy whom other boys like; A boy who is at ease in the company of girls;
A boy who is not sorry for himself, and not forever thinking and talking about himself;
A boy who is friendly with his mother, and more intimate with her than anyone else;
A boy who makes you feel good when he is around;
A boy who is not just healthy, happy, and full of life.
This boy is wanted everywhere.
The family wants him,
The school wants him,
The office wants him,
The boys want him,
The girls want him,
All creation wants him!

For Everything There Is a Season

For everything there is a season, and a time for every purpose under the heaven:
A time to be born and a time to die;
A time to plant, and a time to pluck up that which is planted;
A time to kill, and a time to heal;
A time to break down, and a time to build up;
A time to weep, and a time to laugh;
A time to mourn, and a time to dance;
A time to cast away stones, and a time to gather stones together;

A time to embrace, and a time to refrain from embracing;
A time to get, and a time to lose; a time to keep, and a time to cast away;
A time to rend, and a time to sew; a time to keep silence, and a time to speak;
A time to love, and a time to hate; a time of war, and a time of peace.

COMPASSION

Just as courage takes its stand by others in challenging situations, so compassion takes its stand with others in their distress. Compassion is a virtue that takes seriously the reality of other persons, their inner lives, their emotions, as well as their external circumstances. It is an active disposition toward fellowship and sharing, toward supportive companionship in distress or in woe.

The seeds of compassion are sown in our very nature as human beings. Compassion is a natural feeling, which, by moderating the violence of love of self in each individual, contributes to the preservation of the whole species. It is this compassion that hurries us without reflection to the relief of those who are in distress.

Compassion seeks to retain our hold on this very early awareness that we are all in the same boat, that "but for the grace of God there go I." **Compassion** thus comes close to the very heart of moral awareness, to seeing in one's neighbour another self.

Kindness to Animals

Compassion may be first learned through kindness to all creatures great and small.
Little children, never give pain to things that feel and live;
    Let the gentle robin come for the crumbs you save at home;
        As his meat you throw along;
        He'll repay you with a song.
    Never hurt the timid hare peeping from her green grass lair,
    Let her come and sport and play on the lawn at close of day.
    The little lark goes soaring high to the bright windows of the sky,
        Singing as if 'twere always spring,
        And fluttering on an untired wing—

> Oh! Let him sing his happy song,
> Nor do these gentle creatures wrong.

The Lion and the Mouse

Aesop

Here is one of the oldest and best—loved stories of kindness paid and repaid. From it we learn that compassion lies within the power of both the mighty and the meek. **Kindness** *is not a feeble virtue.*

One day a great lion lay asleep in the sunshine. A little mouse ran across his paw and wakened him. The great lion was just going to eat him up when the little mouse cried, "Oh, please, let me go, sir. Someday I may help you." The lion laughed at the thought that the little mouse could be of any use to him. But he was a good-natured lion, and he set the mouse free. Not long after, the lion was caught in a net. He tugged and pulled with all his might, but the ropes were too strong. Then he roared loudly. The little mouse heard him, and ran to the spot. "Be still, dear Lion, and I will set you free. I will gnaw the ropes." With his sharp little teeth, the mouse cut the ropes, and the lion came out of the net. "You laughed at me once," said the mouse. "You thought I was too little to do you a good turn. But see, you owe your life to a poor little mouse."

Little Sunshine

Bestowing compassion is like offering most other gifts. Often it's the thought that counts.

Once there was a little girl named Elsa. She had a very old grandmother, with white hair, and wrinkles all over her face. Elsa's father had a large house that stood on a hill. Each day the sun peeped in at the south windows. It made everything look bright and beautiful. The grandmother lived on the north side of the house. The sun never came to her room. One day Elsa said to her father, "Why doesn't the sun peep into Grandma's room? I know she would like to have him." "The sun cannot look in at the north windows," said her father. "Then let us turn the house around, Papa." "It is much too large for that," said her father.

"Will Grandma never have any sunshine in her room?" asked "Of course not, my child, unless you can carry some to her." After that

Elsa tried and tried to think how she could carry the sunshine to her grandmother. When she played in the fields she saw the grass and the flowers nodding their heads. The birds sang sweetly as they flew from tree to tree. Everything seemed to say, "We love the sun. We love the bright, warm sun." "Grandma would love it, too," thought the child. "I must take some to her."

When she was in the garden one morning she felt the sun's warm rays in her golden hair. Then she sat down and she saw them in her lap. "I will take them in my dress," she thought, "and carry them to Grandma's room." So she jumped up and ran into the house. "Look, Grandma, Look! I have some sunshine for you," she cried. And she opened her dress, but there was not a ray to be seen. "It peeps out of your eyes, my child," said her grandmother, "and it shines in your sunny, golden hair. I do not need the sun when I have you with me." Elsa did not understand how the sun could peep out of her eyes. But she was glad to make her dear grandmother happy. Every morning she played in the garden. Then she ran to her grandmother's room to carry the sunshine in her eyes and hair.

A Child's Prayer
God make my life a little light,
Within the world to glow;
A tiny flame that burn bright
Wherever I may go.
God make my life a little flower,
That gives joy to all,
Content to bloom in native bower,
Although it's place be small.
God make my life a little song,
That comforts the sad;
That helps others to be strong,
And makes the singer glad.
God make my life a little staff,
Whereon the weak may rest,
That so what health and strength I have
May serve my neighbour's best.

Androcles and the Lion

This ancient story is another, more slightly complicated version of the fable of the Lion and the Mouse. Here the human element is introduced. Its appeal lies in the fact that Androcles the slave can feel compassion at another's pain even though he himself has been so cruelly mistreated. It is a unique human capacity, to be able to put oneself in the place and point of view of another. In the end, his kindness sets him free.

In Rome there was once a poor slave whose name was Androcles. His master was a cruel man, and so unkind to him that at last Androcles ran away. He hid himself in a wild wood for many days. But there was no food to be found, and he grew so weak and sick that he thought he would die. So one day he crept into a cave and lay down, and soon he was fast asleep. After a while a great noise woke him up. A lion had come into the cave, and was roaring loudly. Androcles was very much afraid, for he felt sure that the beast would kill him. Soon, however, he saw that the lion was not angry, but that he limped as though his foot hurt him. Then Androcles grew so bold that he took hold of the lion's lame paw to see what was the matter. The lion stood quite still, and rubbed his head against the man's shoulder. He seemed to say "I know that you will help me." Androcles lifted the paw from the ground, and saw that it was a long, sharp thorn which hurt the lion so much. He took the end of the thorn in his fingers; then he gave a strong, quick pull, and out it came. The lion was full of joy. He jumped about, like a dog, and licked the hands and feet of his new friend. Androcles was not at all afraid after this. And when night came, he and the lion lay down and slept side by side. For a long time, the lion brought food to Androcles every day, and the two became such good friends that Androcles found his new life a very happy one.

One day some soldiers who were passing through the wood found Androcles in the cave. They knew who he was, and so took him back to Rome. It was the law at that time that every slave who ran away from his master should be made to fight a hungry lion. So a fierce lion was shut up for a while without food, and a time *was set for the fight. When the day came, thousands of people crowded to see the sport. They went to such places at that time very much as people now go to see a circus show, or a game of baseball.

The door opened, and poor Androcles was brought in. He was almost dead with fear, for the roars of the lion could already be heard. He looked up, and saw that there was no pity in the thousands of faces around him. Then the hungry lion rushed in. With a single bound he reached the poor slave. Androcles gave a great cry, not of fear, but of gladness. It was his old friend, the lion of the cave. The people, who had expected to see the man killed by the lion, were filled with wonder. They saw Androcles put his arms around the lion's neck; they saw the lion lie down at his feet, and lick them lovingly; they saw the great beast rub his head against the slave's face as though he wanted to be petted. They could not understand what it all meant.

After a while they asked Androcles to tell them about it. So he stood up before them, and, with his arm around the lion's neck, told how he and the beast had lived together in the cave. "I am a man," he said, "but no man has ever befriended me. This poor lion alone has been kind to me and we love each other as brothers." The people were not so bad that they could be cruel to the poor slave now. "Live and be free!" they cried. "Live and be free!"

Others cried, "Let the lion go free too! Give both of them their liberty!" And so Androcles was set free, and the lion was given to him for his own. And they lived together in Rome for many years.

Little Thumbelina

This story is a shortened version of Hans Christian Andersen's "Thumbelina." Like the fable of the Lion and the Mouse, it teaches little children **how to have large hearts**.

Once upon a time there was a little girl no bigger than her Mother's thumb, and so they called her "Thumbelina."

Thumbelina did not sleep in a little white bed, as you do; her bed was half of a walnut shell. Her Mother covered her with pink rose leaves for blankets when she curled up for a cozy nap. By and by, when Thumbelina had grown large enough to run about wherever she wished to go, she started for a walk one beautiful sunny morning. She had not gone very far when she heard something coming hoppity-skip, hoppity-skip behind her. She turned around, and there she saw a great big green Grasshopper. "How do you do, Thumbelina?" he said. "Wouldn't you like to go for a ride this morning?"

"I should like it very much," said Thumbelina. "Very well, hop up on my back," said the Grasshopper. So Thumbelina hopped up on his back, and away they went, hoppity-skip, hoppity-skip, through the grass. Thumbelina thought it was the finest ride she had ever had. After a while the Grasshopper stopped and let her get down off his back. "Thank you, Mr. Grasshopper," said Thumbelina. "It was very good of you to take me for a ride." "I'm glad you enjoyed it," said the Grasshopper. "You may go again some day. Goodbye." And away he went, hoppity-skip, hoppity-skip, through the grass, while Thumbelina went on her walk. She walked on and on until she came to a river, and as she stood on the bank, looking down into the shining water, a Fish came swimming up. "How do you do, Thumbelina?" he said. "How do you do, Mr. Fish?" said Thumbelina. "Wouldn't you like to go for a sail this morning?" asked the Fish. "Yes, indeed," said Thumbelina, "but there is no boat." "Wait a moment," said the Fish, and he flirted his tail, and darted away through the water. Presently he came swimming back to the bank, and in his mouth he held the stem of a lily leaf. "Step down on this; it will make a fine boat." Thumbelina stepped down on the lily leaf and sat carefully in the middle of it. The Fish kept the stem in his mouth, and swam away down the stream. Overhead the birds were singing, along the bank the flowers were blooming, and over the edge of the leaf Thumbelina could see the fish darting here and there through the water. So they sailed and sailed down the river. But at last the Fish took her back to the bank again. "Thank you for the sail, Mr. Fish," Thumbelina said as she stepped off onto the bank. "I never had such a good time in all my life." "I'm glad you enjoyed it, Thumbelina. Goodbye for today." The Fish darted away through the water, and Thumbelina turned to go home. Just then Mrs. Mouse came running up. "How do you do, Thumbelina?" she said. "Won't you come home with me and see my babies?" "I'd love to," said Thumbelina, and she clapped her hands in glee. Mrs. Mouse's home was quite a way down under the ground. Thumbelina crept through the long dark passageway to the cozy room in which Mrs. Mouse and her three babies lived. They all ran races up and down the long passageway, and Thumbelina tasted the dried peas which Mrs. Mouse had brought home with her. "I think I must go home now," Thumbelina said at last. "My Mother will be wondering where I am." So she said goodbye to them all and started off home.

    She had not walked very far along the path through the field when she heard something saying "Peep, peep" in a weak, sick little voice. Thumbelina looked, and there close beside her in the grass she saw a little Bird. His eyes were shut, and he looked very sick. "Why, what's the matter, little Bird?" said Thumbelina. "Oh, I have a thorn in my foot, and it does hurt so.""Let me see," said Thumbelina. "Perhaps I can help you." She looked carefully, and there she saw the thorn sticking in the poor Bird's foot. She took her little fingers and pulled it out, as gently as she could. Then she fetched some clear, cold water and bathed the wounded foot. The Bird felt so much better that he opened his eyes. "Why, it is Thumbelina!" he said. "How did you know my name?" said Thumbelina, in surprise. "That's easy to explain," said the Bird. "My nest is up in a tree, close beside your window. I often hear your Mother calling you. But are you not a long way from home?" "Yes, I am," said Thumbelina. "I was hurrying home when I found you." "Well," said the Bird, "if you climb up on my back, I'll take you there, far more quickly than you can run." So Thumbelina climbed up on the Birdie's back. "Hold on tight," he said, as he spread his wings and flew swiftly up above the treetops. He went so high that sometimes they skimmed along through the clouds, and so fast that Thumbelina could hardly get her breath; but still she thought it was very wonderful, and she was not a bit afraid. Soon the Bird sat right in the window of Thumbelina's own room. She climbed down off his back, and thanked him for bringing her home. Then she ran away to find her Mother, and tell her all about the wonderful things which had been happening to her that day.

Beautiful

Socrates believed beauty is a thing that "slips in and permeates our souls."

Beautiful faces are they that wear
The light of a pleasant spirit there;
Beautiful hands are they that do
Deeds that are noble, good and true;
Beautiful feet are they that go
Swiftly to lighten another's woe.

Song of Life

The Roman statesman **Seneca** *wrote that wherever there is a human being, there is an opportunity for a kindness. No selfless act is insignificant.*

A traveller on a dusty road
Strewed acorns on the lea;
And one took root and sprouted up,
And grew into a tree.
Love sought its shade at evening time,
To breathe its early vows;
And Age was pleased, in heights of noon,
To bask beneath its boughs.
The dormouse loved its dangling twigs,
The birds sweet music bore— It stood a glory in its place,
A blessing evermore.
A little spring had lost its way
Amid the grass and fern;
A passing stranger scooped a well
Where weary men might turn.
He walled it in, and hung with care
A ladle on the brink;
He thought not of the deed he did,

But judged that toil might drink.
He passed again; and lo! the well,
By summer never dried,
Had cooled ten thousand parched tongues,
And saved a life beside.
A nameless man, amid the crowd
That thronged the daily mart,
Let fall a word of hope and love,
Unstudied from the heart,
A whisper of the tumult thrown,
A transitory breath,
It raised a brother from the dust,
It saved a soul from death.
0 germ! O fount!
0 word of love!
0 thought at random cast!
Ye were but little at the first,
But mighty at the last.

If I Can Stop One Heart from Breaking

Emily Dickinson

Emily Dickinson (1830—1886) reminds us that acts of ***compassion*** *add meaning to our lives.*
If I can stop one heart from breaking,
I shall not live in vain;
If I can ease one life the aching,
Or cool one pain,
Or help one fainting robin
Unto his nest again,
I shall not live in vain.

Echo and Narcissus

In Greek mythology, Narcissus was a beautiful youth, the son of the river Cephisus and the nymph Leiriopa. His vanity and heartlessness have made his name forever synonymous with intense self-infatuation. Self-absorption often makes compassion impossible, and vice versa.

Echo was a beautiful nymph, fond of the woods and hills, where she devoted herself to woodland sports. She was a favorite of Diana, and attended her in the chase. But Echo had one failing; she was fond of talking, and whether in chat or argument, would have the last word.

One day Juno was seeking her husband, who, she had reason to fear, was amusing himself among the nymphs. Echo by her talk contrived to detain the goddess till the nymphs made their escape. When Juno discovered it, she passed sentence upon Echo in these words: "You shall forfeit the use of that tongue with which you have cheated me, except for that one purpose you are so fond of a reply. You shall still have the last word, but no power to speak first."

This nymph saw Narcissus, a beautiful youth, as he pursued the chase upon the mountains. She loved him and followed his footsteps. O how she longed to address him in the softest accents, and win him to converse! But it was not in her power. She waited with impatience for him to speak first, and had her answer ready. One day the youth, being separated from his companions, shouted aloud, "Who's here?" Echo replied, "Here." Narcissus looked around, but seeing no one, called out, "Come." Echo answered, "Come." As no one came, Narcissus called again, "Why do you shun me?" Echo asked the same question. "Let us join one another," said the youth. The maid answered with all her heart in the same words, and hastened to the spot, ready to throw her arms about his neck. He started back, exclaiming, "Hands off! I would rather die than you should have me!" "Have me," said she; but it was all in vain. He left her, and she went to hide her blushes in the recesses of the woods. From that time forth she lived in caves and among mountain cliffs. Her form faded with grief, till at last all her flesh shrank away. Her bones were changed into rocks and there was nothing left of her but her voice. With that she is still ready to reply to anyone who calls her, and keeps up her old habit of having the last word.

Narcissus's cruelty in this case was not the only instance. He shunned all the rest of the nymphs, as he had done poor Echo.

One day a maiden who had in vain endeavored to attract him uttered a prayer that he might sometime or other feel what it was to love and meet no return of affection. The avenging goddess heard and granted the prayer. There was a clear fountain, with water like silver, to which the shepherds never drove their flocks, nor the mountain goats resorted, nor any of the beasts of the forests; neither was it defaced with fallen leaves or branches; but the grass grew fresh around it, and the rocks sheltered it from the sun.

    Hither came one day the youth, fatigued with hunting, heated and thirsty. He stooped down to drink, and saw his own image in the water; he thought it was some beautiful water spirit living in the fountain. He stood gazing with admiration at those bright eyes, those locks curled like the locks of Bacchus or Apollo, the rounded cheeks, the ivory neck, the parted lips, and the glow of health and exercise over all. He fell in love with himself. He brought his lips near to take a kiss; he plunged his arms in to embrace the beloved object. It fled at the touch, but returned again after a moment and renewed the fascination. He could not tear himself away. He lost all thought of food or rest, while he hovered over the brink of the fountain gazing upon his own image. He talked with the supposed spirit. "Why, beautiful being, do you shun me? Surely my face is not one to repel you. The nymphs love me, and you yourself look not indifferent upon me. When I stretch forth my arms you do the same; and you smile upon me and answer my beckonings with the like."

His tears fell into the water and disturbed the image. As he saw it depart, he exclaimed, "Stay, I entreat you! Let me at least gaze upon you, if I may not touch you." With this, and much more of the same kind, he cherished the flame that consumed him, so that by degrees he lost his color, his vigor, and the beauty which formerly had so charmed the nymph Echo. She kept near him, however, and when he exclaimed, "Alas! Alas!" she answered him with the same words. He pined away and died; and when his shade passed the Stygian river, it leaned over the boat to catch a look of itself in the waters. The nymphs mourned for him, especially the water nymphs; and when they smote their breasts Echo smote hers also. They prepared a funeral pyre and would have burned the body, but it was nowhere to be found; but in its place a flower, purple within, and surrounded with white leaves, which bears the name and preserves the memory of Narcissus.

0 Captain! My Captain!

Walt Whitman

Here Walt Whitman mourns for the fallen Abraham Lincoln. To the poet, the assassination was a terrible blow to the American democratic comradeship he celebrated in so much of his verse. Repeated metaphorical reference is made to this issue throughout the verse. The "ship" spoken of is intended to represent the **United States of America**, while its "fearful trip" recalls the troubles of the **American Civil War.** The **titular** "Captain" is Lincoln himself.

0 Captain! my Captain! our fearful trip is done;
The ship has weather'd every rack, the prize we sought is won;
The port is near, the bells I hear, the people all exulting,
While follow eyes the steady keel, the vessel grim and daring:

But 0 heart! heart! heart!
0 the bleeding drops of red,
Where on the deck my Captain lies,
Fallen cold and dead.

0 Captain! my Captain! rise up and hear the bells;
Rise up—for you the flag is flung—for you the bugle trills;
For you bouquets and ribbon'd wreaths—for
you the shores a-crowding;
For you they call, the swaying mass, their eager faces turning:
Here Captain! dear father!
This arm beneath your head! It is some dream that on the deck,
You've fallen cold and dead.

My Captain does not answer, his lips are pale and still;
My father does not feel my arm, he has no pulse nor will;
The ship is anchor'd safe and sound, its voyage closed and done;
From fearful trip, the victor ship comes in with object won:
Exult, 0 shores, and ring, 0 bells!
But I, with mournful tread,
Walk the deck my Captain lies,
Fallen cold and dead.

Over in the Meadow

Olive A. Wadsworth

*This poem shows us **parents' first responsibility: the nurture of the young.***

Over in the meadow,
In the sand, in the sun,
Lived an old mother toad
And her little toadie one.
"Wink," said the mother;
"I wink," said the one;
So she winked and she blinked In the sand, in the sun.
Over in the meadow,
Where the stream runs blue,
Lived an old mother fish
And her little fishes two.
"Swim," said the mother;
"We swim," said the two;
So they swam and they leaped
Where the stream runs blue.
Over in the meadow,
In a hole in a tree,
Lived an old mother bluebird
And her little birdies three.
"Sing," said the mother;
"We sing," said the three;
So they sang and were glad,
In the hole in the tree.
Over in the meadow,
In the reeds on the shore,
Lived a mother musk rat
And her little ratties four.
"Dive," said the mother;
"We dive," said the four;
So they dived and they burrowed
In the reeds on the shore.

Rebecca

Play is the work of children and entirely suitable as an arena in which to develop habits of responsibility.

I have a doll, Rebecca,
She's quite a little care,
I have to press her ribbons
And comb her fluffy hair.
I keep her clothes all mended,
And wash her hands and face,
And make her frocks and aprons,
All trimmed in frills and lace.
I have to cook her breakfast,
And pet her when she's ill;
And telephone the doctor
When Rebecca has a chill.
Rebecca doesn't like that,
And says she's well and strong;
And says she'll try—oh! very hard,
To be good all day long.
But when night comes, she's nodding;
So into bed we creep
And snuggle up together,
And soon are fast asleep.
I have no other dolly,
For you can plainly see,
In caring for Rebecca,
I'm busy as can be!

The Boy We Want

A boy that is truthful and honest and faithful and willing to work;
But we have not a place that we care to disgrace
With a boy that is ready to shirk.
Wanted—a boy you can tie to,
A boy that is trusty and true,
A boy that is good to old people,
And kind to the little ones too.
A boy that is nice to the home folks,
And pleasant to sister and brother,
A boy who will try when things go awry
To be helpful to father and mother.
These are the boys we depend on—
Our hope for the future, and then grave
problems of state and the world's work await
Such boys when they grow to be men.

Etiquette in a Nutshell

This little list of rules comes from a Handbook of Etiquette.
These are some of the day-to-day commonplace obligations that allow us to get along with one another. They never go out of style.

Never break an engagement when one is made, whether of a business or social nature.

If you are compelled to do so, make an immediate apology either by note or in person.

Be punctual as to time, precise as to payment, honest and thoughtful in all your transactions, whether with rich or poor.

Never look over the shoulder of one who is reading, or intrude yourself into a conversation in which you are not invited or expected to take part.

Tell the truth at all times and in all places.

It is better to have a reputation for truthfulness than one for wit, wisdom, or brilliancy.

Avoid making personal comments regarding a person's dress, manners, or habits.

Be sure you are all right in these respects, and you will find you have quite enough to attend to.

Always be thoughtful regarding the comfort and pleasure of others.

Give the best seat in your room to a lady, an aged person, or an invalid.

Ask no questions about the affairs of your friend unless he wants your advice.

Then he will tell you all he desires to have you know.

A true lady or gentleman, one who is worthy of the name, will never disparage one of the other sex by word or deed.

Always remember that a book that has been loaned you is not yours to loan to another.

Mention your wife or your husband with the greatest respect, even in your most familiar references.

If you have calls to make, see that you attend to them punctually.

Your friends may reasonably think you slight them when you fail to do so.

Be neat and careful in your dress, but take care not to overdress. **The fop is almost as much of an abomination** as the slovenly man.
If wine or liquors are used on your table or in your presence, never urge others to use them against their own inclinations.

If You Were

*This little poem reminds us whose responsibilities
we should take care of first.*

If you were busy being kind,
Before you knew it, you would find
You'd soon forget to think 'twas true
That someone was unkind to you.
If you were busy being glad,
And cheering people who are sad,
Although your heart might ache a bit,
You'd soon forget to notice it.
If you were busy being good,
And doing just the best you could,
You'd not have time to blame some man
Who's doing just the best he can.
If you were busy being right,
You'd find yourself too busy quite
To criticize your neighbour long
      Because he's busy being wrong.

IF

"**If**—" is a poem written in 1895 by British Nobel laureate Rudyard Kipling

Brave men and women (as well as cowardly men and women) are not born that way; they become that way through their acts. Here are the acts that make us not just grow up, but grow up well.

If you can keep your head when all about you
Are losing theirs and blaming it on you;
If you can trust yourself when all men doubt you,
But make allowance for their doubting too:
If you can wait and not be tired by waiting,
Or being lied about, don't deal in lies,
Or being hated, don't give way to hating,
And yet don't look too good, nor talk too wise;

If you can dream—and not make dreams your master;
If you can think—and not make thoughts your aim,
If you can meet with Triumph and Disaster
And treat those two impostors just the same:
If you can bear to hear the truth you've spoken
Twisted by knaves to make a trap for fools,
Or watch the things you gave your life to, broken,
And stoop and build 'em up with worn-out tools;

If you can make one heap of all your winnings
And risk it on one turn of pitch-and-toss,
And lose, and start again at your beginnings
And never breathe a word about your loss:
If you can force your heart and nerve and sinew
To serve your turn long after they are gone,
And so hold on when there is nothing in you
Except the Will which says to them: "Hold on!"

If you can talk with crowds and keep your virtue,
Or walk with Kings—nor lose the common touch,
If neither foes nor loving friends can hurt you,
If all men count with you, but none too much:
If you can fill the unforgiving minute
With sixty seconds' worth of distance run,
Yours is the Earth and everything that's in it,
And—which is more—**you'll be a Man, my son!**

Icarus and Daedalus

This famous Greek myth reminds us exactly why young people have a responsibility to obey their parents—for the same good reason parents have a responsibility to guide their children: there are many things adults know that young people do not. The ancient Greek dramatist Aeschylus put it this way: **"Obedience is the mother of success and is wedded to safety."** *Safe childhoods and successful upbringings require a measure of obedience, as Icarus finds out the hard way.*

Daedalus was the most skillful builder and inventor of his day in ancient Greece. He built magnificent palaces and gardens, and created wonderful works of art throughout the land. His statues were so beautifully crafted they were taken for living beings, and it was believed they could see and walk about. People said someone as cunning as Daedalus must have learned the secrets of his craft from the gods themselves.

Now across the sea, on the island of Crete, lived a king named Minos. King Minos had a terrible monster that was half bull and half man called the Minotaur, and he needed someplace to keep it. When he heard of Daedalus's cleverness, he invited him to come to his country and build a prison to hold the beast. So Daedalus and his young son, Icarus, sailed to Crete, and there Daedalus built the famous Labyrinth, a maze of winding passages so tangled and twisted that whoever went in could never find the way out. And there they put the Minotaur. When the Labyrinth was finished, Daedalus wanted to sail back to Greece with his son, but Minos had made up his mind to keep them in Crete. He wanted Daedalus to stay and invent more wonderful devices for him, so he locked them both in a high tower beside the sea. The king knew Daedalus was clever enough to escape from the tower, so he also ordered that every ship be searched for stowaways before sailing from Crete. Other men may have given up, but not Daedalus. From his high tower he watched the seagulls drifting on the ocean breezes. "Minos may control the land and the sea," he said, "but he does not rule the air. We'll go that way." So he summoned all the secrets of his craft, and he set to work. Little by little, he gathered a great pile of feathers of all sizes. He fastened them together with thread, and molded them with wax, and at last he had two great wings like those of the seagulls. He tied them to his shoulders, and after one or two clumsy efforts, he found that by waving his arms he could rise into the air. He held himself alof wavering this way and that with the wind, until he taught himself how to glide and soar on the currents as gracefully as any gull. Next he built a second pair of wings for Icarus. He taught the boy how to move the feathers and rise a few feet into the air, and then let him fly back and forth across the room. Then he taught him how to ride the air currents, climbing in circles, and hang in the winds. They practiced together until Icarus was ready.

Finally, the day came when the winds were just right. Father and son strapped on their wings and prepared to fly home. "Remember all I've told you," Daedalus said. "Above all? remember you must not fly too high or too low. If you fly too low, the ocean sprays will clog your wings and make them too heavy. If you fly too high, the heat of the sun will melt the wax, and your wings will fall apart. Stay close to me, and you'll be fine." Up they rose, the boy after his father, and the hateful ground of Crete sank far beneath them. As they flew the plowman stopped his work to gaze, and the shepherd leaned on his staff to watch them, and people came running out of their houses to catch a glimpse of the two figures high above the treetops. Surely they were gods— Apollo, perhaps, with Cupid after him.

At first the flight seemed terrible to both Daedalus and Icarus. The wide, endless sky dazed them, and even the quickest glance down made their brains reel. But gradually they grew used to riding among the clouds, and they lost their fear. Icarus felt the wind fill his wings and lift him higher and higher, and began to sense a freedom he had never known before. He looked down with great excitement at all the islands they passed, and their people, and at the broad blue sea spread out beneath him, dotted with the white sails of ships. He soared higher and higher, forgetting his father's warning. He forgot everything in the world but joy. Come back Daedalus called frantically. "You're flying too high! Remember the sun! Come down! Come down!" But Icarus thought of nothing but his own excitement and glory. He longed to fly as close as he could to the heavens. Nearer and nearer he came to the sun, and slowly his wings began to soften. One by one the feathers began to fall and scatter in the air, and suddenly the wax melted all at once. Icarus felt himself falling. He fluttered his arms as fast as he could, but no feathers remained to hold the air. He cried out for his father, but it was too late—with a scream he fell from his lofty height and plunged into the sea, disappearing beneath the waves. Daedalus circled over the water again and again, but he saw nothing but feathers floating on the waves, and he knew his son was gone. At last the body came to the surface, and he managed to pluck it from the sea. With a heavy burden and broken heart, Daedalus slowly flew away. When he reached land, he buried his son and built a temple to the gods. Then he hung up his wings, and never flew again.

The Duties of a Scout

In his original book on boy scouting, Baden-Powell introduced the Scout Promise, as follows:
Before he becomes a scout, a boy must take the scout's oath, thus:
On my honour I promise that---
While taking this oath the scout will stand, holding his right hand raised level with his shoulder, palm to the front, thumb resting on the nail of the digitus minimus (little finger) and the other three fingers upright, pointing upwards:--- This is the scout's salute and secret sign.
Here are the rules every Boy Scout and Girl Scout promises to live by. Other than the Ten Commandments, it is hard to imagine a better list of virtuous aims for the young.

The Boy Scout Oath
On my honor

I will do my best to do my duty to God and my country
and to obey the Scout Law;
To help other people at all times;
To keep myself physically strong,
Mentally awake,
And morally straight.

The Girl Scout Promise
On my honor, I will try:

To serve God and my country,
To help people at all times, And to live by the
Girl Scout Law.

A Scout is Trustworthy
A Scout is Loyal
A Scout is Helpful
A Scout is Friendly
A Scout is Courteous
A Scout is Kind
A Scout is Obedient
A Scout is Cheerful
A Scout is Thrifty
A Scout is Brave
A Scout is Clean
A Scout is Reverent

The Boy Scout Law

I will do my best:

- to be honest
- to be fair
- to help where I am needed
- to be cheerful
- to be friendly and considerate
- to be a sister to every Girl Scout
- to respect authority
- to use resources wisely
- to protect and improve the world around me
- to show respect for myself and others through my words and actions

What a Baby Costs

Edgar Guest

It is never too early to begin impressing upon our children, by both word and deed, the responsibilities of parenthood. Part of the job of raising children is raising them to be successful parents themselves.

"How much do babies cost?" said he
The other night upon my knee;
And then I said: "They cost a lot;
A lot of watching by a cot,
A lot of sleepless hours and care,
A lot of heartache and despair,
A lot of fear and trying dread,
And sometimes many tears are shed
In payment for our babies small,
But everyone is worth it all.
"For babies people have to pay
A heavy price from day to day—
There is no way to get one cheap.
Why, sometimes when they're fast asleep
You have to get up in the night
And go and see that they're all right.
But what they cost in constant care
And worry, does not half compare.
With what they bring of joy and bliss—
You'd pay much more for just a kiss.
"Who buys a baby has to pay
A portion of the bill each day;
He has to give his time and thought
Unto the little one he's bought.
He has to stand a lot of pain
Inside his heart and not complain;
And pay with lonely days and sad
For all the happy hours he's had.
All this a baby costs, and yet
His smile is worth it all, you bet."

His Daughter
F. Scott Fitzgerald

In this letter we see the molding of character: a father gently but explicitly telling his daughter what her duties are.

Dear Pie:

I feel very strongly about your doing duty. Would you give me a little more documentation about your reading in French? I am glad you are happy—but I never believe much in happiness. I never believe in misery either. Those are things you see on the stage or the screen or the printed page, they never really happen to you in life. All I believe in life is the rewards for virtue (according to your talents) and the punishments for not fulfilling your duties, which are doubly costly. If there is such a volume in the camp library, will you ask Mrs. Tyson to let you look up a sonnet of Shakespeare's in which the line occurs: "Lilies that fester smell far worse than weeds."

Have had no thoughts today, life seems composed of getting up a Saturday Evening Post story. I think of you, and always pleasantly; but if you call me "Pappy" again I am going to take the White Cat out and beat his bottom hard, six times for every time you are impertinent. Do you react to that? I will arrange the camp bill. Halfwit, I will conclude.

Things to worry about:
Worry about courage
Worry about cleanliness
Worry about efficiency
Worry about horsemanship
Things not to worry about:
Don't worry about popular opinion
Don't worry about dolls
Don't worry about the past
Don't worry about the future
Don't worry about growing up
Don't worry about anybody getting ahead of you
Don't worry about triumph
Don't worry about failure unless it comes through your own fault
Don't worry about mosquitoes
Don't worry about flies

Don't worry about insects in general
Don't worry about parents
Don't worry about boys
Don't worry about disappointments
Don't worry about pleasures
Don't worry about satisfactions

Things to think about: What am I really aiming at? How good am I in comparison to my contemporaries in regard to: (a) Scholarship (b) Do I really understand about people and am I able to get along with them? (c) Am I trying to make my body a useful instrument or am I neglecting it?

With dearest love

The Pasture

Robert Frost

*This little poem reminds us that a friend is someone
we want to be with.*

I'm going out to clean the pasture spring;
   I'll only stop to rake the leaves away
   (And wait to watch the water clear, I may):
I shan't be gone long.—You come too.
   I'm going out to fetch the little calf
     That's standing by the mother.
       It's so young,
It totters when she licks it with her tongue.
I shan't be gone long.—**You come too.**

Stopping By Woods on a Snowy Evening
Robert Frost

Whose woods these are I think I know.
His house is in the village though;
He will not see me stopping here
To watch his woods fill up with snow.

My little horse must think it queer
To stop without a farmhouse near
Between the woods and frozen lake
The darkest evening of the year.

He gives his harness bells a shake
To ask if there is some mistake.
The only other sound's the sweep
Of easy wind and downy flake.

The woods are lovely, dark and deep.
But I have promises to keep,
And miles to go before I sleep,
And miles to before I sleep.

The Bear and the Travellers
Aesop

Fair-weather friends were around in the days of Aesop, in the sixth century B.C., and they still abound today. Children should learn how to recognize one, and how not to be one.

Two Travellers were on the road together, when a Bear suddenly appeared on the scene. Before he observed them, one made for a tree at the side of the road, and climbed up into the branches and hid there. The other was not so nimble as his companion; and, as he could not escape, he threw himself on the ground and pretended to be dead. The Bear came up and sniffed all round him, but he kept perfectly still and held his breath; for they say that a bear will not touch a dead body. The Bear took him for a corpse, and went away. When the coast was clear, the Traveller in the tree came down, and asked the other what it was the Bear had whispered to her, when he put his mouth to her ear. The other replied, "He told me never again to travel with a friend who deserts you at the first sign of danger."

Misfortune tests the sincerity of friendship.

Cat and Mouse in Partnership
The Brothers Grimm

As this story shows us, picking the wrong friend can be disappointing or even disastrous.

A cat having made acquaintance with a mouse, professed such great love and friendship for her, that the mouse at last agreed that they should live and keep house together.

"We must make provision for the winter," said the cat, "or we shall suffer hunger, and you, little mouse, must not stir out, or you will be caught in a trap."

So they took counsel together and bought a little pot of honey.

And then they could not tell where to put it for safety, but after long consideration the cat said there could not be a better place than the church, for nobody would steal there, and they would put it under the altar and not touch it until they were really in want. So this was done, and the little pot placed in safety.

But before long the cat was seized with a great wish to taste it. "Listen to me, little mouse," said he, "I have been asked by my cousin to stand godfather to a little son she has brought into the world. He is white with brown spots. And they want to have the christening today, so let me go to it, and you stay at home and keep house."

"Oh yes; certainly," answered the mouse, "pray go by all means. And when you are feasting on all the good things, think of me. I should so like a drop of the sweet red wine."

But there was not a word of truth in all this. The cat, had no cousin, and had not been asked to stand godfather. He went to the church, straight up to the little pot, and licked the honey off the top. Then he took a walk over the roofs of the town, saw his acquaintances, stretched himself in the sun, and licked his whiskers as often as he thought of the little pot of honey.

And then when it was evening he went home. "Here you are at last," said the mouse. "I expect you have had a merry time." "Oh, pretty well," answered the cat. "And what name did you give the child?" asked the mouse. "Top-off," answered the cat, dryly. "Top-off!" cried the mouse. "That is a singular and wonderful name! Is it common in your family?" "What does it matter?" said the cat. "It's not any worse than Crumb-picker, like your godchild." A little time after this the cat was again seized with a longing. "Again I must ask you," said he to the mouse, "to do me a favour, and keep house alone for a day. I have been asked a second time to stand godfather. And as the little one has a white ring around its neck, I cannot well refuse."

So the kind little mouse consented, and the cat crept along by the town wall until he reached the church, and going straight to the little pot of honey, devoured half of it. "Nothing tastes so well as what one keeps to oneself," said he, feeling quite content with his day's work. When he reached home, the mouse asked what name had been given to the child. "Half—gone," answered the cat. "Half—gone!" cried the mouse.

"I never heard such a name in my life! I'll bet it's not to be found in the calendar." Soon after that the cat's mouth began to water again for the honey. "Good things always come in threes," said he to the mouse. "Again I have been asked to stand godfather, the little one is quite black with white feet, and not any white hair on its body. Such a thing does not happen every day, so you will let me go, won't you?" "Top-on, Half-gone," murmured the mouse. " They are such curious names, I cannot but wonder at them!" "That's because you are always sitting at home," said the cat, "in your little gray frock and hairy tail, never seeing the world, and fancying all sorts of things." So the little mouse cleaned up the house and set it all in order. Meanwhile the greedy cat went and made an end of the little pot of honey. "Now all is finished one's mind will be easy," said he, and came home in the evening, quite sleek and comfortable. The mouse asked at once what name had been given to the third child. "It won't please you any better than the others," answered the cat. "It is called All—gone." "All-gone!" cried the mouse. "What an unheard-of name! I never met with anything like it! All-gone! Whatever can it mean?" And shaking her head, she curled herself round and went to sleep. After that the cat was not again asked to stand godfather. When the winter had come and there was nothing more to be had out of doors, the mouse began to think of their store. "Come, cat," said she, "we will fetch our pot of honey, how good it will taste, to be sure!"

"Of course, it will," said the cat. So they set out, and when they reached the place, they found the pot, but it was standing empty. "Oh, now I know what it all meant," cried the mouse, "now I see what sort of a partner you have been! Instead of standing godfather you have devoured it all, first Top-off, then Half-gone, then—" "Will you hold your tongue!" screamed the cat. "Another word, and I'll devour you too!"

And the poor little mouse having "All-gone" on her tongue, out it came, and the cat leaped upon her and made an end of her.

And that is the way of the world.

Friendship

This poem reminds us of some of the "rules" of friendship, as well as some of the rewards.

Friendship needs no studied phrases,
Polished face, or winning wiles;
Friendship deals no lavish praises,
Friendship dons no surface smiles.
Friendship follows Nature's diction,
Shuns the blandishments of art,
Boldly severs truth from fiction,
Speaks the language of the heart.
Friendship favors no condition,
Scorns a narrow-minded creed,
Lovingly fulfills its mission,
Be it word or be it deed.
Friendship cheers the faint and weary,
Makes the timid spirit brave,
Warns the erring, lights the dreary,
Smooths the passage to the grave.
Friendship—pure, unselfish friendship,
All through life's allotted span,
Nurtures, strengthens, widens, lengthens,
Man's relationship with man.

A Wayfaring Song

Henry van Dyke

O who will walk a mile with me
Along life's merry way?
A comrade blithe and full of glee,
Who dares to laugh out loud and free
And let his frolic fancy play,
Like a happy child, through the flowers gay
That fill the field and fringe the way
Where he walks a mile with me.

And who will walk a mile with me
Along life's weary way?
A friend whose heart has eyes to see
The stars shine out o'er the darkening lea,
And the quiet rest at the end o' the day—
A friend who knows, and dares to say,
The brave, sweet words that cheer the way
Where he walks a mile with me.

With such a comrade, such a friend,
I fain would walk till journey's end,
Through summer sunshine, winter rain,
And then?—
Farewell, we shall meet again!

The Human Touch
Spencer Michael Free

This simple poem reminds us that genuine friendship is about the closeness of hands, hearts, and souls. It also, incidentally, captures the profundity of "touch" between Helen Keller and Anne Mansfield Sullivan.

'Tis the human touch in this world that counts,
The touch of your hand and mine,
Which means far more to the fainting heart
Than shelter and bread and wine;
For shelter is gone when the night is o'er,
And bread lasts only a day,
But the touch of the hand and the sound of the voice
Sing on in the soul always.

A Time to Talk

Robert Frost

Work always calls us.
But we make time for friends when they call too.
When a friend calls to me from the road
And slows his horse to a meaning walk,
I don't stand still and look around
On all the hills I haven't hoed,
And shout from where I am, What is it?
No, not as there is a time to talk.
I thrust my hoe in the mellow ground,
Blade—end up and five feet tall,
And plod: I go up to the stone wall
For a friendly visit.

The Song of the Bee

Marian Douglas

This poem set the tone for work in school and life.

God seems to have created bees to inspire us toward industry.
Buzz! buzz! buzz!
This is the song of the bee.
His legs are of yellow;
A jolly, good fellow,
And yet a great worker is he.
In days that are sunny
He's getting his honey;
In days that are cloudy
He's making his wax:
On pinks and on lilies,
And gay daffodillies,
And columbine blossoms,
He levies a tax!

Buzz! buzz! buzz!
Makes fragrant his wings:
He never gets lazy;
From thistle and daisy,
And weeds of the meadow,
Some treasure he brings.
Buzz! buzz! buzz!
From morning's first light
Till the coming of night,
He's singing and toiling
The summer day through.
Oh! we may get weary,
And think work is dreary;
**'Tis harder by far
To have nothing to do.**

Five Little Chickens

Said the first little chicken,

With a queer little squirm,
"Oh, I wish I could find
A fat little worm!"
Said the next little chicken,
With an odd little shrug,
"Oh, I wish I could find
A fat little bug!"
Said the third little chicken,
With a sharp little squeal,
"Oh, I wish I could find
Some nice yellow meal!"
Said the fourth little chicken,
'With a small sigh of grief,

"Oh, I wish I could find
A green little leaf"
Said the fifth little chicken,
With a faint little moan,
"Oh, I wish I could find
A wee gravel-stone!"
"Now, see here," said the mother,
From the green garden-patch,
"If you want any breakfast,
You must come and scratch."

The Ants and the Grasshopper

Aesop

The ant, like the bee, has long been held up as a paradigm of industriousness. As Proverbs 6:6—8 in the Bible says, "Go to the ant, thou sluggard; consider her ways and be wise: which having no guide, overseer, or ruler, provideth her meal in the summer, and gathereth her food in the harvest."

One fine day in winter some ants were busy drying their store of corn, which had got rather damp during a long spell of rain. Presently up came a grasshopper and begged them to spare her a few grains. "For," she said, "I'm simply starving." The ants stopped work for a moment, though this was against their principles. "May we ask," said they, "what you were doing with yourself all last summer? Why didn't you collect a store of food for the winter?" "The fact is," replied the grasshopper, "I was so busy singing that I hadn't the time." "If you spent the summer singing," replied the ants, "you can't do better than spend the winter dancing." And they chuckled and went on with their work.

Work While You Work

This poem is a good one for those modern souls who turn on the TV while they're doing their homework, or spend more time at the coffee machine than at their desk. On the other hand, it's also a good one for those who can't bring themselves to venture onto a beach or into a movie theater without taking their beepers with them.

> Work while you work,
> Play while you play;
> One thing each time,
> That is the way.
> All that you do,
> Do with your might;
> **Things done by halves**
> **Are not done right.**

Hercules and the Wagoner
Aesop

Some people exhibit an almost miraculous resolve in waiting for someone else to come along and do their work for them. This old fable may help us learn early that the only certain labor is your own.

A wagoner was driving his team along a muddy lane with a full load behind them, when the wheels of his wagon sank so deep in the mire that no efforts of his horses could move them. As he stood there, looking helplessly on, and calling loudly at intervals upon Hercules for assistance, the god himself appeared, and said to him, "Put your shoulder to the wheel, man, and goad on your horses, and then you may call on Hercules to assist you. If you won't lift a finger to help yourself, you can't expect Hercules or anyone else to come to your aid."

Heaven helps those who help themselves.

Mr. Meant-To

Hear the famous words of Benjamin Franklin: "Work while it is called today, for you know not how much you may be hindered tomorrow. One today is worth two tomorrows; never leave that till tomorrow which you can do today."

Mr. Meant-Too has a comrade,
And his name is Didn't-Do;
Have you ever chanced to meet them?
Did they ever call on you?
These two fellows live together
In the house of Never-Win,
And I'm told that it is haunted
By the **ghost of Might-Have-Been**.

The Farmer and His Sons

Aesop

A farmer, being at death's door, and desiring to impart to his sons a secret of much moment, called them round him and said, "My sons, I am shortly about to die. I would have you know, therefore, that in my vineyard there lies a hidden treasure. Dig, and you will find it." As soon as their father was dead, the sons took spade and fork and turned up the soil of the vineyard over and over again, in their search for the treasure which they supposed to lie buried there.

They found none, however: but the vines, after so thorough a digging, produced a crop such as had never before been seen. **There is no treasure without toil.**

What Have We Done Today?
Nixon Waterman

Work is not a plan for work.
Putting off work can be the same as just
plain not working.
We shall do much in the years to come,
But what have we done today?
We shall give our gold in a princely sum,
But what did we give today?
We shall lift the heart and dry the tear,
We shall plant a hope in the place of fear,
We shall speak the words of love and cheer,
But what did we speak today?
We shall be so kind in the after while,
But have we been today?
We shall bring to each lonely life a smile,
But what have we brought today?
We shall give to truth a grander birth,
And to steadfast faith a deeper worth,
We shall feed the hungering souls of earth,
But whom have we fed today?
We shall reap such joys in the by and by,
But what have we sown today?
We shall build us mansions in the sky,
But what have we built today?
'Tis sweet in the idle dreams to bask;
But here and now, do we our task?
Yet, this is the thing our souls must ask,
What have we done today?

I Meant to Do My Work Today
Richard Le Gallienne

This little poem is a reminder that, as the saying goes, "All work and no play makes Jack a dull boy." But we should also remember that we enjoy play the most when it crowns good, hard work.

I meant to do my work today,
But a brown bird sang in the apple tree,
And a butterfly flitted across the field,
And all the leaves were calling me.
And the wind went sighing over the land,
Tossing the grasses to and fro,
And a rainbow held out its shining hand—
So what could I do but laugh and go?

The Bundle of Sticks

Aesop

A certain man had several sons who were always quarrelling with one another, and, try as he might, he could not get them to live together in harmony. So he determined to convince them of their folly by the following means. Bidding them fetch a bundle of sticks, he invited each in turn to break it across his knee. All tried and all failed: and then he undid the bundle, and handed them the sticks one by one, when they had no difficulty at all in breaking them. "There, my boys," said he, "united you will be more than a match for your enemies: but if you quarrel and separate, your weakness will put you at the mercy of those who attack you."

Union is strength.

Results and Roses
Edgar Guest

The man who wants a garden fair,
Or small or very big,
With flowers growing here and there,
Must bend his back and dig.
The things are mighty few on earth
That wishes can attain.
Whate'er we want of any worth
We've got to work to gain.
It matters not what goal you seek
Its secret here reposes:
You've got to dig from week to week
To get
Results or Roses.

Opportunity

John James Ingalls

"There is a tide in the affairs of men," William Shakespeare wrote, "which, taken at the flood, leads on to fortune." The catch is that opportunity almost always involves some breasting of the tide—i.e., hard work. Many people would rather simply wait for their ship to come in.

Master of human destinies am I!
Fame, love, and fortune on my footsteps wait.
Cities and fields I walk;
I penetrate Deserts and seas remote, and passing by
Hovel and mart and palace—soon or late
I knock unbidden once at every gate!
If sleeping, wake—
If feasting, rise before I turn away.

It is the hour of fate,
And they who follow me reach every state
Mortals desire, and conquer every foe
Save death; but those who doubt or hesitate,
Condemned to failure, penury and woe,
Seek me in vain and uselessly implore.
I answer not, and I return no more!

Heaven Is Not Reached in a Single Bound

J. G. Holland

Heaven is not reached at a single bound,
But we build the ladder by which we rise
From the lowly earth to the vaulted skies,
And we mount to its summit round by round.
I count this thing to be grandly true:
That a noble deed is a step toward God—
Lifting the soul from the common clod
To a purer air and a broader view.

Great Men

Ralph Waldo Emerson

Not gold, but only man can make
A people great and strong;
Men who, for truth and honour's sake,
Stand fast and suffer long.
Brave men who work while others sleep,
Who dare while others fly—
They build a nation's pillars deep
And lift them to the sky.

Success

Henry Wadsworth Longfellow

These lines are from Longfellow's "The Ladder of Saint Augustine."

We have not wings, we cannot soar;
But we have feet to scale and climb
By slow degrees, by more and more,
The cloudy summits of our time.
The mighty pyramids of stone
That wedge—like cleave the desert airs,
When nearer seen, and better known,
Are but gigantic flights of stairs.
The distant mountains, that uprear
Their solid bastions to the skies,
Are crossed by pathways, that appear
As we to higher levels rise.
The heights by great men reached and kept
Were not attained by sudden flight,
But they, while their companions slept,
Were toiling upward in the night.

The Noble Nature

If we devote care to details, our work will shine in small bits
and pieces—and our characters will improve degree by degree.

It is not growing like a tree
In bulk, doth make man better be;
Or standing long an oak, three hundred year,
To fall a log at last, dry, bald, and sear:
A lily of a day
Is fairer far in May,
Although it fall and die that night—
It was the plant and flower of Light.
In small proportions we just beauties see,
And in short measures life may perfect be.

A Psalm of Life
Henry Wadsworth Longfellow

Henry Wadsworth Longfellow said of this poem: "I kept it sometime in manuscript, unwilling to show it to anyone, it being a voice from my inmost heart, at a time when I was rallying from depression." The verse reminds us that work is often the best cure for unhappiness. Another great American writer and contemporary of Longfellow, Nathaniel Hawthorne, gives the same prescription in The Scarlet Letter: "Preach! Write! Act! Do anything, save to lie down and die!"

Tell me not, in mournful numbers,
Life is but an empty dream!—
For the soul is dead that slumbers,
And things are not what they seem.

Life is real! Life is earnest!
And the grave is not its goal;
Dust thou art, to dust returnest,
Was not spoken of the soul.

Not enjoyment, and not sorrow,
Is our destined end or way;
But to act, that each tomorrow
Find us farther than today.

Art is long, and Time is fleeting,
And our hearts, though stout and brave,
Still, like muffled drums, are beating
Funeral marches to the grave.

In the world's broad field of battle,
In the bivouac of Life,
Be not like dumb, driven cattle!
Be a hero in the strife!

Trust no Future, howe'er pleasant!
Let the dead Past bury its dead!
Act—act in the living Present!

Heart within, and God o'erhead!
Lives of great men all remind us
We can make our lives sublime,
And, departing, leave behind us
Footprints on the sands of time;
Footprints, that perhaps another,
Sailing o'er life's solemn main,
A forlorn and shipwrecked brother,
Seeing, shall take heart again.
Let us, then, be up and doing,
With a heart for any fate;
Still achieving, still pursuing,
Learn to labour and to wait.

How the Little Kite Learned to Fly

It's amazing how much of the world's virtue comes from one little word: "Try." Trying something for the first time often calls for bravery. "Try, try again," on the other hand, requires that sibling virtue: perseverance

"I never can do it," the little kite said,
As he looked around at the others high over his head.
"I know I should fall if I tried to fly."
"Try," said the big kite, "only try!
Or I fear you never will learn at all."
But the little kite said, "I'm afraid I'll fall."
The big kite nodded: "Ah well, goodbye; I'm off,"
and he rose toward the tranquil sky.
Then the little kite's paper stirred at the sight,
And trembling he shook himself free for flight.
First whirling and frightened, then braver grown,
Up, up he rose through the air alone,
Till the big kite looking down could see
The little one rising steadily.
Then how the little kite thrilled with pride,

As he sailed with the big kite side by side!
While far below he could see the ground,
And the boys like small spots moving round.
They rested high in the quiet air,
And only the birds and the clouds were there.
**"Oh, how happy I am!" the little kite cried,
"And all because I was brave, and tried."**

The Brave Mice

Aesop

Saying you'll do something may take one kind of courage, but actually doing it requires a different type. Real bravery lies in deeds, not words.

An old cat was in the habit of catching all the mice in the barn. One day the mice met to talk about the great harm that she was doing them. Each one told of some plan by which to keep out of her way. "Do as I say," said an old gray mouse that was thought to be very wise. "Do as I say. Hang a bell to the cat's neck. Then, when we hear it ring, we shall know that she is coming, and can scamper out of her way." "Good! good!" said all the other mice, and one ran to get the bell. "Now which of you will hang this bell on the cat's neck?" said the old gray mouse. "Not I! Not I!" said all the mice together. And they scampered away to their holes.

Compensation

Theodosia Garrison

Teddy Roosevelt said that "far better it is to dare mighty things, to win glorious triumphs, even though checkered by failure, than to take rank with those poor spirits who neither enjoy much nor suffer much, because they live in the gray twilight that knows neither victory nor defeat." This poem reminds us as well that a mighty heart reaches high.

Because I craved a gift too great

For any prayer of mine to bring,
Today with empty hands I go;
Yet must my heart rejoice to know
I did not ask a lesser thing.
Because the goal I sought lay far In cloud-hid heights,
Today my soul Goes unaccompanied of its own;
Yet this shall comfort me alone,
I did not seek a nearer goal.
0 gift ungained, 0 goal unwon!
Still am I glad, remembering this,
For all I go unsatisfied,
I have kept faith with joy denied,
Nor cheated life with cheaper bliss.

Doors of Daring

Henry van Dyke

Barriers are invitations to courage.
The mountains that enclose the vale
With walls of granite, steep and high,
Invite the fearless foot to scale
Their stairway toward the sky.
The restless, deep, dividing sea
That flows and foams from shore to shore,
Calls to its sunburned chivalry, "Push out, set sail, explore!"
The bars of life at which we fret,
That seem to prison and control,
Are but the doors of daring, set
Ajar before the soul.
Say not, "Too poor," but freely give;
Sigh not, "Too weak," but boldly try;
You never can begin to live
Until you dare to die.

William Tell

This famous story of the legendary Swiss hero William Tell takes place in the early part of the fourteenth century, during the Swiss people's struggle for independence from Austrian rule. It is one of our greatest tales of cool and calm bravery in the face of bullying tyranny.

The people of Switzerland were not always free and happy as they are today. Many years ago a proud tyrant, whose name was Gessler, ruled over them, and made their lot a bitter one indeed. One day this tyrant set up a tall pole in the public square, and put his own cap on the top of it; and then he gave orders that every man who came into the town should bow down before it. But there was one man, named William Tell, who would not do this. He stood up straight with folded arms, and laughed at the swinging cap. He would not bow down to Gessler himself. When Gessler heard of this, he was very angry. He was afraid that other men would disobey, and that soon the whole country would rebel against him. So he made up his mind to punish the bold man. William Tell's home was among the mountains, and he was a famous hunter. No one in all the land could shoot with bow and arrow so well as he. Gessler knew this, and so he thought of a cruel plan to make the hunter's own skill bring him to grief. He ordered that Tell's little boy should be made to stand up in the public square with an apple on his head; and then he bade Tell shoot the apple with one of his arrows. Tell begged the tyrant not to have him make this test of his skill. What if the boy should move? What if the bowman's hand should tremble? What if the arrow should not carry true? "Will you make me kill my boy?" he said. "Say no more," said Gessler. "You must hit the apple with your one arrow. If you fail, my soldiers shall kill the boy before your eyes." Then, without another word, Tell fitted the arrow to his bow. He took aim, and let it fly. The boy stood firm and still. He was not afraid, for he had all faith in his father's skill. The arrow whistled through the air.

It struck the apple fairly in the center, and carried it away. The people who saw it shouted with joy. As Tell was turning away from the place, an arrow which he had hidden under his coat dropped to the ground. "Fellow!" cried Gessler, "what mean you with this second arrow?" "Tyrant!" as Tell's proud answer, "this arrow was for your heart if I had hurt my child." And there is an old story, that not long after this, Tell did shoot the tyrant with one of his arrows, and thus he set his country free.

The Things That Haven't Been Done Before

Edgar Guest

The ones who dared to do
What we now take for granted are the ones we remember.
The things that haven't been done before,
Those are the things to try;
Columbus dreamed of an unknown shore
At the rim of the far-flung sky,
And his heart was bold and his faith was strong
As he ventured in dangers new,
And he paid no heed to the jeering throng
Or the fears of the doubting crew.
The many will follow the beaten track
With guideposts on the way.
They live and have lived for ages back
With a chart for every day.
Someone has told them it's safe to go on
the road he has traveled o'er,
And all that they ever strive to know
Are the things that were known before.
A few strike out, without map or chart,
Where never a man has been,
From the beaten paths they draw apart
To see what no man has seen.
There are deeds they hunger alone to do;
Though battered and bruised and sore,
They blaze the path for the many,

Who do nothing not done before.
The things that haven't been done before
Are the tasks worthwhile today;
Are you one of the flock that follows, or
Are you one that shall lead the way?
Are you one of the timid souls that quail
At the jeers of a doubting crew,
Or dare you, whether you win or fail,
Strike out for a goal that's new?

The Road Not Taken

Robert Frost

Two roads diverged in a yellow wood,
And sorry I could not travel both
And be one traveler, long I stood
And looked down one as far as I could
To where it bent in the undergrowth;

Then took the other, as just as fair,
And having perhaps the better claim
Because it was grassy and wanted wear,
Though as for that the passing there
Had worn them really about the same,

And both that morning equally lay
In leaves no step had trodden black.
Oh, I marked the first for another day!
Yet knowing how way leads on to way
I doubted if I should ever come back.

I shall be telling this with a sigh
Somewhere ages and ages hence:
Two roads diverged in a wood, and I,
I took the one less traveled by,
And that has made all the difference.

A Smile

*Those who fight the good fight and win need to be
brave only once. Those who lose must
show courage twice. So we must steel ourselves
for harder things than triumph.*

Let others cheer the winning man,
There's one I hold worthwhile;
'Tis he who does the best he can,
Then loses with a smile.
Beaten he is, but not to stay
Down with the rank and file;
**That man will win some other day,
Who loses with a smile.**

The Rainy Day

Henry Wadsworth Longfellow

*Life calls for a variety of everyday fortitudes. They may be less
spectacular than the valour of a hazardous climax, but they
nevertheless determine what kind of students, spouses, parents,
workers, and citizens we are. Facing life's realities, its downs
as well as its ups, is one kind of daily courage we all must learn.*

The day is cold, and dark, and dreary;
It rains, and the wind is never weary;
The vine still clings to the moldering wall,
But at every gust the dead leaves fall,
And the day is dark and dreary.
My life is cold, and dark, and dreary;
It rains, and the wind is never weary;
My thoughts still cling to the moldering Past,
But the hopes of youth fall thick in the blast,
And the days are dark and dreary.
Be still, sad heart! and cease repining;
Behind the clouds is the sun still shining;
Thy fate is the common fate of all,
Into each life some rain must fall,
Some days must be dark and dreary.

Persevere

The fisherman who draws in his net too soon,
Won't have any fish to sell;
The child who shuts up his book too soon,
Won't learn any lessons well.
If you would have your learning stay,
Be patient—don't learn too fast;
The man who travels a mile each day,
May get round the world at last.

The Tortoise and the Hare

Aesop

As Aesop knew, perseverance makes up for all sorts of disadvantages. Here is a case of virtue outdistancing undisciplined ability.

A hare once made fun of a tortoise. "What a slow way you have!" he said. "How you creep along!" Do I?" said the tortoise. "Try a race with me and I'll beat you." "What a boaster you are," said the hare. "But come! I will race with you. Whom shall we ask to mark off the finish line and see that the race is fair?" "Let us ask the fox," said the tortoise. The fox was very wise and fair. He showed them where they were to start, and how far they were to run. he tortoise lost no time. He started out at once and jogged straight on. Tie hare leaped along swiftly for a few minutes till he had left the tortoise far behind. He knew he could reach the mark very quickly, so he lay down by the road under a shady tree and took a nap. By and by he awoke and remembered the race. He sprang up and ran as fast as he could. But when he reached the mark the tortoise was already there! "Slow and steady wins the race," said the fox.

A hare and a tortoise story... the modern version!

Once upon a time a tortoise and a hare had an argument about who was faster.

They decided to settle the argument with a race. They agreed on a route and started off the race.

The hare shot ahead and ran briskly for some time.

Then seeing that he was far ahead of the tortoise, he thought he'd sit under a tree for some time and relax before continuing the race. He sat under the tree and soon fell asleep.

The tortoise plodding on overtook him and soon finished the race, emerging as the undisputed champ.

The hare woke up and realized that he'd lost the race.

The **moral**- "Slow and steady wins the race. This is the version of the story that we've all grown up with."

THE STORY DOESN'T END HERE
there are few more interesting
things......it continues as follows......

The hare was disappointed at losing the race and he did some soul-searching.

He realized that he'd lost the race only because he had been overconfident, careless and lax.

If he had not taken things for granted, there's no way the tortoise could have beaten him. So he challenged the tortoise to another race.

The tortoise agreed. This time, the hare went all out and ran without stopping from start to finish. He won by several miles.

The **moral** - " Fast and consistent will always beat the slow and steady.

It's good to be slow and steady; but it's better to be fast and reliable."

THE STORY DOESN'T END HERE

The tortoise did some thinking this time, and realized that there's no way it can beat the hare in a race the way it was currently formatted.

It thought for a while, and then challenged the hare to another race, but on a slightly different route. The hare agreed. They started off. In keeping with his self-made commitment to be consistently fast, the hare took off and ran at top speed until he came to a broad river. The finishing line was a couple of kilometres on the other side of the river.

The hare sat there wondering what to do.

In the meantime the tortoise trundled along, got into the river, swam to the opposite bank, continued walking and finished the race.

The **moral** - "First identify your core competency and then change the playing field to suit your core competency."

THE STORY STILL HASN'T ENDED

The hare and the tortoise, by this time, had become pretty good friends and they did some thinking together.

Both realized that the last race could have been run much better So they decided to do the last race again, but to run as a team this time.

They started off, and this time the hare carried the tortoise till the riverbank. There, the tortoise took over and swam across with the hare on his back. On the opposite bank, the hare again carried the tortoise and they reached the finishing line together. They both felt a greater sense of satisfaction than they'd felt earlier.

The **moral** - "It's good to be individually brilliant and to have strong core competencies; but unless you're able to work in a team and harness each other's core competencies, you'll always perform below par because there will always be situations at which you'll do poorly and someone else does well."

Teamwork is mainly about situational leadership, letting the person with the relevant core competency for a situation take leadership. Note that neither the hare nor the tortoise gave up after failures. The hare decided to work harder and put in more effort after his failure. The tortoise changed his strategy because he was already working as hard as he could."

In life, when faced with failure, sometimes it is appropriate to work harder and put in more effort.

The Crow and the Pitcher

Aesop

This is the famous fable from Aesop which tells us that where there's a will accompanied by practical intelligence, there's a way.

Once there was a thirsty crow. She had flown a long way looking for water to drink. Suddenly she saw a pitcher. She flew down and saw it held a little water, but it was so low in the pitcher that she could not reach it. But I must have that water, she cried. I am too weary to my farther. What shall I do? I know! I'll tip the pitcher over." She beat it with her wings, but it was too heavy. She could not move it. Then she thought awhile. "I know now! I will break it! Then I will drink the water as it pours out. How good it will taste!" With beak and claws and wings she threw herself against the pitcher. But it was too strong. The poor crow stopped to rest. "What shall I do now? I cannot die of thirst with water close by. There must be a way, if I only had wit enough to find it out." After a while the crow had a bright idea. There were many small stones lying about. She picked them up one by one and dropped them into the pitcher. Slowly the water rose, till at last she could drink it. How good it tasted! "There is always a way out of hard places," said the crow, "if only you have the wit to find it."

You Mustn't Quit

When things go wrong, as they sometimes will,
When the road you're trudging seems all uphill,
When the funds are low and the debts are high
And you want to smile, but you have to sigh,
When care is pressing you down a bit,
Rest! if you must—but never quit.
Life is queer, with its twists and turns,
As every one of us sometimes learns,
And many a failure turns about
When he might have won if he'd stuck it out;
Stick to your task, though the pace seems slow—
You may succeed with one more blow.
Success is failure turned inside out—
The silver tint of the clouds of doubt—
And you never can tell how close you are,
It may be near when it seems afar;
So stick to the fight when you're hardest hit—
It's when things seem worst that YOU MUSTN'T QUIT.

Solitude

Ella Wheeler Wilcox

Sometimes we persevere with the help and compassion of friends and loved ones. Sometimes we have to do it alone. This poem speaks a hard truth, but one we might as well accept nonetheless: pain is harder to share than joy. But if we can bring ourselves to endure cheerfully, we'll find more company along the way.

Laugh, and the world laughs with you;
Weep, and you weep alone;
For the sad old earth must borrow its mirth,
But has trouble enough of its own.
Sing, and the hills will answer;
Sigh, it is lost on the air;
The echoes bound to a joyful sound,
But shrink from voicing care.

Rejoice, and men will seek you;
Grieve, and they turn and go;
They want full measure of all your pleasure,
But they do not need your woe.
Be glad, and your friends are many;
Be sad, and you lose them all—
There are none to decline your nectared wine,
But alone you must drink life's gall.
Feast, and your halls are crowded;
Fast, and the world goes by.
Succeed and give, and it helps you live,
But no man can help you die.
There is room in the halls of pleasure
For a large and lordly train,
But one by one we must all file on
Through the narrow aisles of pain.

Bruce and the Spider
Bernard Barton

Robert Bruce (1274—1329) was the king of Scotland who freed his land from English rule by winning the Battle of Bannockburn (1314) and ultimately confirming Scottish independence in the Treaty of Northampton (1328). But the fight was long and hard, as this famous story, set to verse, tells.

For Scotland's and for freedom's right
The Bruce his part had played,
In five successive fields of fight
Been conquered and dismayed;
Once more against the English host
His band he led, and once more lost
The meed for which he fought;
And how from battle, faint and worn,
The homeless fugitive forlorn
A hut's lone shelter sought.
And cheerless was that resting place
For him who claimed a throne:

His canopy, devoid of grace,
The rude, rough beams alone;
The heather couch his only bed—
Yet well I ween had slumber fled
From couch of eiderdown!
Through darksome night till dawn of day,
Absorbed in wakeful thoughts he lay of
Scotland and her crown.
The sun rose brightly, and its gleam
Fell on that hapless bed,
And tinged with light each shapeless beam
Which roofed the lowly shed;
When, looking up with wistful eye,
The Bruce beheld a spider try
His filmy thread to fling
From beam to beam of that rude cot;
And well the insect's toilsome lot
Taught Scotland's future king.
Six times his gossamery thread
The wary spider threw;
In vain the filmy line was sped,
For powerless or untrue
Each aim appeared, and back recoiled
The patient insect, six times foiled,
And yet unconquered still;
And soon the Bruce, with eager eye,
Saw him prepare once more to try
His courage, strength, and skill.
One effort more, his seventh and last-
The hero hailed the sign!—
And on the wished-for beam hung fast
That slender, silken line!
Slight as it was, his spirit caught
The more than omen, for his thought
The lesson well could trace,
Which even "he who runs may read,"
That Perseverance gains its meed,
And Patience wins the race.

Can't

Edgar Guest

"Can't" is a favourite word of some children. Here is the case against it.

Can't is the worst word that's written
or spoken;
Doing more harm here than slander and lies;
On it is many a strong spirit broken,
And with it many a good purpose dies.
It springs from the lips of the
thoughtless each morning
And robs us of courage we need through the day:
It rings in our ears like a timely sent warning
And laughs when we falter and fall by the way.
Can't is the father of feeble endeavor,
The parent of terror and halfhearted work;
It weakens the efforts of artisans clever,
And makes of the toiler an indolent shirk.
It poisons the soul of the man with a vision,
It stifles in infancy many a plan;
It greets honest toiling with open derision
And mocks at the hopes and the dreams of a man.
Can't is a word none should speak without blushing;
To utter it should be a symbol of shame;
Ambition and courage it daily is crushing;
It blights a man's purpose and shortens his aim.
Despise it with all of your hatred of error;
Refuse it the lodgment it seeks in your brain;
Arm against it as a creature of terror,
And all that you dream of you someday shall gain.
Can't is the word that is foe to ambition,
An enemy ambushed to shatter your will;
Its prey is forever the man with a mission
And bows but to courage and patience and skill.
Hate it, with hatred that's deep and undying,
For once it is welcomed 'twill break any man;
Whatever the goal you are seeking, keep
trying and answer this demon by saying: "**I can.**"

Will
Ella Wheeler Wilcox

There is no chance, no destiny, no fate, that can
circumvent or hinder or control
The firm resolve of a determined soul.
Gifts count for nothing; will alone is great;
All things give way before it, soon or late.
What obstacle can stay the mighty force of the
sea—seeking river in its course,
Or cause the ascending orb of day to wait?
Each well-born soul must win what it deserves.
Let the fool prate of luck.
The fortunate is he whose earnest purpose never swerves,
Whose slightest action or inaction serves
The one great aim.
Why, even Death stands still,
And waits an hour sometimes for such a will.

The Boy Who Never Told a Lie

An honest heart will always find friends.

Once there was a little boy,
With curly hair and pleasant eye—.
A boy who always told the truth,
And never, never told a lie.
And when he trotted off to school,
The children all about would cry,
"There goes the curly-headed boy— The boy that never tells a lie."
And everybody loved him so,
Because he always told the truth,

> That every day, as he grew up,
> 'Twas said, "There goes the honest youth."
> And when the people that stood near
> Would turn to ask the reason why,
> The answer would be always this:
> "Because he never tells a lie."

The Boy Who Cried "Wolf"

Aesop

This may be Aesop's most famous fable, and for good reason. The fastest way to lose what we call our "good character" is to lose our honesty.

There was once a shepherd boy who kept his flock at a little distance from the village. Once he thought he would play a trick on the villagers and have some fun at their expense. So he ran toward the village crying out, with all his might: "Wolf. Wolf. Come and help! The wolves are at my lambs!" The kind villagers left their work and ran to the field to help him. But when they got there the boy laughed at them for their pains; there was no wolf there. Still another day the boy tried the same trick, and the villagers came running to help and were laughed at again. Then one day a wolf did break into the fold and began killing the lambs. In great fright, the boy ran back for help. "Wolf. Wolf." he screamed. "There is a wolf in the flock! Help!" The villagers heard him, but they thought it was another mean trick; no one paid the least attention, or went near him. And the shepherd boy lost all his sheep. That is the kind of thing that happens to people who lie: even when they do tell the truth they will not be believed.

Someone Sees You

This folktale reminds us that an act of dishonesty is never truly hidden.

Once upon a time a man decided to sneak into his neighbor's fields and steal some wheat. "If I take just a little from each field, no one will notice," he told himself, "but it will all add up to a nice pile of *heat for me." So he waited for the darkest night, when thick clouds lay over the moon, and he crept out of his house. He took his youngest daughter with him. "Daughter," he whispered, "you must stand guard, and call out if anyone sees me." The man stole into the first field to begin reaping, and before long the child called out, "Father, someone sees you!" The man looked all around, but he saw no one, so he gathered his stolen wheat and moved on to a second field. "Father, someone sees you!" the child cried again. The man stopped and looked all around, but once again he saw no one. He gathered more wheat, and moved to a third field. A little while passed, and the daughter cried out, "Father, someone sees you!" Once more the man stopped his work and looked in every direction, but he saw no one at all, so he bundled his wheat and crept into the last field. "Father, someone sees you!" the child called again. The man stopped his reaping, looked all around, and once again saw no one. "Why in the world do you keep saying someone sees me?" he angrily asked his daughter. "I've looked everywhere, and I don't see anyone." "Father," murmured the child, "Someone sees you from above."

Rebecca's Afterthought

Elizabeth Turner

In this we learn (with relief) of a much happier ending for a little girl who decided to remain steadfastly honest.

Yesterday, Rebecca Mason,
In the parlor by herself,
Broke a handsome china basin,
Placed upon the mantel shelf.
Quite alarmed, she thought of going
Very quietly away,
Not a single person knowing,
Of her being there that day.
But Rebecca recollected
She was taught deceit to shun;
And the moment she reflected,

> Told her mother what was done;
> Who commended her behavior,
> Loved her better, and forgave her.

Truth, Falsehood, Fire, and Water

This tale about the eternal struggle between truth and falsehood is told in Ethiopia and other eastern African nations.

Long ago Truth, Falsehood, Fire, and Water were journeying together and came upon a herd of cattle. They talked it over and decided it would be fairest to divide the herd into four parts, so each could take home an equal share. But Falsehood was greedy and schemed to get more for himself. "Listen to my warning," he whispered, pulling Water to one side. "Fire plans to burn all the grass and trees along your banks and drive your cattle away across the plains so he can have them for himself. If I were you, I'd extinguish him now, and then we can have his share of the cattle for ourselves." Water was foolish enough to listen to Falsehood, and he dashed himself upon Fire and put him out. Next Falsehood crept toward Truth. "Look what Water has done," he whispered. "He has murdered Fir and taken his cattle. We should not consort with the likes of him. We should take all the cattle and go to the mountains." Truth believed Falsehood and agreed to his plan Together they drove the cattle into the mountains. "Wait for me!" Water called, and he hurried after them, but of course he could not run uphill. So he was left all alone in the valley below. When they reached the top of the highest mountain, Falsehood turned to Truth and laughed. "I've tricked you, stupid fool," he shrieked. "Now you must give me all the cattle and be my servant, or I'll destroy you." "Yes, you have tricked me," Truth admitted, "but I will never be your servant." And so they fought, and when they clashed the thunder rolled back and forth across the mountaintops. Again and again they threw themselves together, but neither could destroy the other. Finally they decided to call upon the Wind to declare a winner of the contest. So Wind came rushing up the mountain slopes, and he listened to what they had to say. "It is not for me to declare a winner in this fight," he told them. "Truth and Falsehood are destined to struggle. Sometimes Truth will win, but other times Falsehood will prevail, and then Truth must rise up and fight again. Until the end of the world, Truth must battle Falsehood, and must never rest or let down his guard, or he will be finished once and for all." And so Truth and Falsehood are fighting to this day.

Truth
Ben Jonson

Ben Jonson (1572—1637) reminds us that faith and love depend on truth.

Truth is the trial of itself,
And needs no other touch;
And purer than the purest gold,
Refine it ne'er so much.
It is the life and light of love,
The sun that ever shineth,
And spirit of that special grace,
That faith and love defineth.
It is the warrant of the word,
That yields a scent so sweet,
As gives a power to faith to tread
All falsehood under feet.

The Question

Seek honesty in yourself before you seek it in your neighbors.

Were the whole world good as you—not an atom better—
Were it just as pure and true, Just as pure and true as you;
Just as strong in faith and works;
Just as free from crafty quirks;
All extortion, all deceit;
Schemes its neighbors to defeat;
Schemes its neighbors to defraud;
Schemes some culprit to applaud— Would
this world be better?
If the whole followed you-followed to the
letter-would it be a nobler world,
All deceit and falsehood hurled from it altogether;
Malice, selfishness, and lust,
Banished from beneath the crust,
Covering human hearts from vie-
Tell me, if it followed you, would the world be better?

Nobility

Alice Cary

This poem brings to mind the words of Alexander Pope:
"An honest man's the noblest work of God."

True worth is in being, not seeming—
In doing, each day that goes by,
Some little good—not in dreaming
Of great things to do by and by.
For whatever men say in their blindness,
And spite of the fancies of youth,
There's nothing so kingly as kindness,
And nothing so royal as truth.

We get back our mete as we measure—
We cannot do wrong and feel right,
Nor can we give pain and gain pleasure,
For justice avenges each slight.
The air for the wing of the sparrow,
The bush for the robin and wren,
But always the path that is narrow
And straight, for the children of men.
'Tis not in the pages of story
The heart of its ills to beguile,
Though he who makes courtship to glory
Gives all that he hath for her smile.
For when from her heights he has won her,
Alas! it is only to prove
That nothing's so sacred as honor,
And nothing so loyal as love!
We cannot make bargains for blisses,
Nor catch them like fishes in nets;
And sometimes the thing our life misses
Helps more than the thing which it gets.
For good lieth not in pursuing,
Nor gaining of great nor of small,
But just in the doing, and doing
As we would be done by, is all.
Through envy, through malice, through hating,
Against the world, early and late,
No jot of our courage abating—
Our part is to work and to wait.
And slight is the sting of his trouble
Whose winnings are less than his worth;
For he who is honest is noble,
Whatever his fortunes or birth.

Truth Never Dies

This poem is inspiring in its assertion that truth is eternal, but perhaps more valuable is its reminder that truth must be "caught and handed onward by the wise." Truth must be passed from friend to friend, from teacher to student, from parent to child.

Truth never dies.
The ages come and go.
The mountains wear away, the stars retire.
Destruction lays earth's mighty cities low;
And empires, states and dynasties expire;
But caught and handed onward by the wise,
Truth never dies.
Though unreceived and scoffed at through the years;
Though made the butt of ridicule and jest;
Though held aloft for mockery and jeers,
Denied by those of transient power possessed,
Insulted by the insolence of lies, Truth never dies.
It answers not.
It does not take offense,
But with a mighty silence bides its time;
As some great cliff that braves the elements
And lifts through all the storms its head sublime,
It ever stands, uplifted by the wise;
And never dies.
As rests the Sphinx amid Egyptian sands;
As looms on high the snowy peak and crest;
As firm and patient as Gibraltar stands,
So truth, unwearied, waits the era blessed
When men shall turn to it with great surprise.
Truth never dies.

Little Boy Blue

Eugene Field

Some of our earliest, most faithful friends are our childhood toys. May we all learn to be as steadfast in our loyalties as the companions of Little Boy Blue.

The little toy dog is covered with dust,
But sturdy and stanch he stands;
And the little toy soldier is red with rust,
And his musket molds in his hands.
Time was when the little toy dog was new
And the soldier was passing fair;
And that was the time when our Little Boy Blue
Kissed them and put them there.
"Now, don't you go till I come," he said,
"And don't you make any noise!"
So, toddling off to his trundle-bed,
He dreamed of the pretty toys;
And as he was dreaming, an angel song
Awakened our Little Boy Blue—
Oh! the years are many, the years are long,
But the little toy friends are true!
Aye, faithful to Little Boy blue they stand,
Each in the same old place—
Awaiting the touch of a little hand,
And the smile of a little face;
And they wonder, as waiting these long years through
In the dust of that little chair,
What has become of our Little Boy Blue,
Since he kissed them and put them there.

Loyalty to a Brother

Walter MacPeek

Family loyalties involve certain obligations. They are duties we perform out of love, as this simple story from an old Boy Scout book reminds us.

One of two brothers fighting in the same company in France fell by a German bullet. The one who escaped asked permission of his officer to go and bring his brother in. "He is probably dead," said the officer, "and there is no use in your risking your life to bring in his body." But after further pleading the officer consented. Just as the soldier reached the lines with his brother on his shoulders, the wounded man died. "There, you see," said the officer, "you risked your life for nothing." "No," replied Tom. "I did what he expected of me, and I have my reward. When I crept up to him and took him in my arms, he said, 'Tom, I knew you would come—I just felt you would come.' There you have the gist of it all; somebody expects something fine and noble and unselfish of us; someone expects us to be faithful.

Only a Dad

Edgar Guest

We should not forget to sing praises for devoted fathers—especially our own. This Edgar Guest poem may help us remember that the only reward a devoted father seeks is his family's flourishing. And may we never forget, as Shakespeare's King Lear told us, "how sharper than a serpent's tooth it is to have a thankless child."

>Only a dad with a tired face,
>Coming home from the daily race,
>Bringing little of gold or fame
>To show how well he has played the game;

But glad in his heart that his own rejoice
To see him come and to hear his voice.
Only a dad with a brood of four,
One of ten million men or more
Plodding along in the daily strife,
Bearing the whips and the scorns of life,
With never a whimper of pain or hate,
For the sake of those who at home await.
Only a dad, neither rich nor proud,
Merely one of the surging crowd,
Toiling, striving from day to day,
Facing whatever may come his way,
Silent whenever the harsh condemn,
And hearing it all for the love of them.
Only a dad but he gives his all,
To smooth the way for his children small,
Doing with courage stern and grim
The deeds that his father did for him.
This is the line that for him I pen:
Only a dad, but the best of men.

The Thousandth Man

Rudyard Kipling

This Kipling poem, which reminds us that loyalty and reliability can sometimes be rare commodities, echoes Ecclesiastes 7:28 in the Bible: "one man in a thousand have I found."

One man in a thousand, Solomon says,
Will stick more close than a brother.
And it's worth while seeking him half your days
If you find him before the other.
Nine hundred and ninety-nine depend

On what the world sees in you,
But the Thousandth Man will stand your friend
With the whole round world again you.
'Tis neither promise nor prayer nor show
Will settle the finding for 'ee.
Nine hundred and ninety-nine of 'em go
By your looks, or your acts, or your glory,
But if he finds you and you find him,
The rest of the world don't matter;
For the Thousandth Man will sink or swim
With you in any water.

You can use his purse with no more talk
Than he uses yours for his spendings,
And laugh and meet in your daily walk
As though there had been no lendings.
Nine hundred and ninety-nine of 'em call
For silver and gold in their dealings;
But the Thousandth Man he's worth 'em all,
Because you can show him your feelings.

His wrong your wrong, and his right's your right,
In season or out of season.
Stand up and back it in all men's sight—
With that for your only reason!
Nine hundred and ninety-nine can't bide
The shame or mocking or laughter,
But the Thousandth Man will stand by your side
To the gallows-foot—and after!

Now I Lay Me Down to Sleep

Say this one every night throughout your adult years.

Now I lay me down to sleep;
I pray the Lord my soul to keep.
If I should die before I wake,
I pray the Lord my soul to take.

A Child's Prayer

Prayer, like all good habits, is best learned
while we are very young.
Lord, teach a little child to pray,
And then accept my prayer;
For thou canst hear the words I say,
For thou art everywhere.
A little sparrow cannot fall
Unnoticed, Lord, by thee;
And though I am so young and small,
Thou dost take care of me.
Teach me to do the thing that's right,
And when I sin, forgive;
And make it still my chief delight
To serve thee while I live.

All Things Beautiful

Cecil Alexander

The miracle of ordinary things fills children's worlds. They sense, as Wordsworth phrased it, the "intimations of immortality" which we too often neglect as adults.

All things bright and beautiful,
All creatures great and small,
All things wise and wonderful,
The Lord God made them all.
Each little flower that opens,
Each little bird that sings,
He made their glowing colours,
He made their tiny wings.
The purple-headed mountain,
The river running by,
The sunset, and the morning,
That brighten up the sky;

The cold wind in the winter,
The pleasant summer sun,
The ripe fruits in the garden,
He made them every one.
The tall trees in the greenwood,
The meadows where we play,
The rushes by the water,
We gather every day;
He gave us eyes to see them,
And lips that we might tell
How great is God Almighty,
Who has made all things well.

I Never Saw a Moor

Emily Dickinson

Faith requires no proofs.
I never saw a moor,
I never saw the sea;
Yet know I how the heather looks,
And what a wave must be.
I never spoke with God,
Nor visited in heaven;
Yet certain am I of the spot
As if the chart were given.

The 23rd Psalm

The book of Psalms was the ancient hymnal of the Jewish people. Most of the psalms were probably written for use in worship; one finds among them songs of praise, thanksgiving, adoration, devotion, doubt, and complaint. Martin Luther called the Psalter "a Bible in miniature." Psalm 23, a hymn of trust in God, is probably the most widely loved.

The Lord is my shepherd;
I shall not want.

He maketh me to lie down in green pastures:
He leadeth me beside the still waters.
He restoreth my soul:
He leadeth me in the paths of righteousness for his name's sake.
Yea, though I walk through the valley of the shadow of death,
I will fear no evil: for thou art with me; thy
rod and thy staff they comfort me.
Thou preparest a table before me in the presence of mine enemies:
Thou anointest my head with oil; my cup runneth over.
Surely goodness and mercy shall follow me all the days of my life:
And I will dwell in the house of the Lord forever.

A Mighty Fortress Is Our God

Martin Luther

This hymn, written by Martin Luther in 1529, has been characterized as "the Battle Hymn of the Reformation." One admirer has noted that "there is something in it like the sound of Alpine avalanches and the first murmur of earthquakes." It is based on Psalm 46.

A mighty fortress is our God,
A bulwark never failing;
Our helper he, amid the flood
Of mortal ills prevailing.
For still our ancient foe
Doth seek to work us woe;
His craft and pow'r are great,
And arm'd with cruel hate,
On earth is not his equal.
Did we in our own strength confide,
Our striving would be losing;
Were not the right man on our side,
The man of God's own choosing.
Dost ask who that may be?
Christ Jesus, it is he;
Lord Sabaoth his name,

From age to age the same,
And he must win the battle.
And though this world, with demons fill'd,
Should threaten to undo us,
We will not fear, for God hath willed
His truth to triumph through us.
The Prince of darkness grim,
We tremble not for him;
His rage we can endure,
For lo, his doom is sure—
One little word shall fell him.
God's word above all earthly pow'rs,
No thanks to them, abideth;
The Spirit and the gifts are ours
Through him who with us sideth.
Let goods and kindred go,
This mortal life also;
The body they may kill;
God's truth abideth still,
His kingdom is forever.

A Name in the Sand

Hannah Flagg Gould

This poem reminds us that we should not overestimate our own importance—except in the eyes of God.

Alone I walked the ocean strand;
A pearly shell was in my hand:
I stooped and wrote upon the sand
My name—the year—the day.
As onward from the spot I passed,
One lingering look behind I cast;
A wave came rolling high and fast,
And washed my lines away.
And so, methought, 'twill shortly be
With every mark on earth from me:

A wave of dark oblivion's sea
Will sweep across the place
Where I have trod the sandy shore of time, and been,
To be no more, of me-my day-the name I bore,
To leave nor track nor trace.
And yet, with him who counts the sands and holds
the waters in his hands,
I know a lasting record stands inscribed against my name,
Of all this mortal part has wrought,
Of all this thinking soul has thought,
And from these fleeting moments
Caught for glory or for shame.

Death, Be Not Proud

John Donne

John Donne's (1572—1631) famous lines insist that death is not the final sleep, but the final awakening.

Death, be not proud, though some have called thee
Mighty and dreadful, for thou are not so;
For those whom thou think'st thou dost overthrow
Die not, poor Death, nor yet canst thou kill me.
From rest and sleep, which but thy pictures be,
Much pleasure—then, from thee much more must flow;
And soonest our best men with thee do go,
Rest of their bones and soul's delivery.
Thou'rt slave to fate, chance, kings, and desperate men,
And dost with poison, war, and sickness dwell;
And poppy or charms can make us sleep as well,
And better than thy stroke.
Why swell'st thou then?
One short sleep past, we wake eternally,
And death shall be no more.
Death, thou shalt die.

Crossing the Bar

Alfred Tennyson

The literal "bar" of this poem is the kind of submerged sandbar that frequently stretches across the mouth of a river or entrance to a harbor. A ship "crosses the bar" when it puts out to sea.

Sunset and evening star,
And one clear call for me!
And may there be no moaning of the bar,
When I put out to sea,
But such a tide as moving seems asleep,
Too full for sound and foam,
When that which drew from out the boundless deep
Turns again home.
Twilight and evening bell,
And after that the dark!
And may there be no sadness of farewell,
When I embark; for though from out our bourne to time and Place
The flood may bear me far, I hope to see my Pilot face—to-face
When I have cross'd the bar.

Last Lines

Emily Bronte

Faith stands firmly rooted in all-pervading love

and life, unshaken by doubt and death.
No coward soul is mine,
No trembler in the world's storm-troubled sphere:
I see Heaven's glories shine,
And faith shines equal, arming me from fear.
O God, within my breast, Almighty, ever-present Deity!
Life—that in me has rest,
As I—undying Life—have power in Thee!
Vain are the thousand creeds

That move men's hearts: unutterably vain;
Worthless as withered weeds,
Or idlest froth amid the boundless main,
To waken doubt in one
Holding so fast by thine infinity;
So surely anchored on
The steadfast rock of immortality.
With wide-embracing love
Thy Spirit animates eternal years,
Pervades and broods above,
Changes, sustains, dissolves, creates, and rears.
Though earth and man were gone,
And suns and universes ceased to be,
And Thou were left alone,
Every existence would exist in Thee.
There is not room for Death,
Nor atom that his might could render void:
Thou—Thou are Being and Breath,
And what Thou art may never be destroyed.

VIRTUE QUOTES

A

Ability

- Whether you think you can or whether you think you can't, you're right!
  Henry Ford *(1863-1947) American industrialist.*

  When love and skill work together, expect a masterpiece.
  John Ruskin *(1819-1900) English art critic.*

  I know of no more encouraging fact than the unquestionable ability of man to elevate his life by conscious endeavor.
  Henry David Thoreau *(1817-1862) American naturalist, poet and philosopher.*

  Big jobs usually go to the men who prove their ability to outgrow small ones.
  Ralph Waldo Emerson *(1803-1882) U.S. poet, essayist and lecturer.*

  The person born with a talent they are meant to use will find their greatest happiness in using it.
  Johann Wolfgang Von Goethe *(1749-1832) German poet, novelist and dramatist.*

  People are so constituted that everybody would rather undertake what they see others do, whether they have an aptitude for it or not.
  Johann Wolfgang Von Goethe *(1749-1832) German poet, novelist and dramatist.*

- Our work is the presentation of our capabilities.
  Johann Wolfgang Von Goethe *(1749-1832) German poet, novelist and dramatist.*

- Life has been compared to a race, but the allusion improves by observing, that the most swift are usually the least manageable and

the most likely to stray from the course. Great abilities have always been less serviceable to the possessors than moderate ones.
Oliver Goldsmith *(1728-1774) Irish writer, poet, and physician.*

- As life is action and passion, it is required of a man that he should share the passion and action of his time, at the peril of being not to have lived.

Oliver Wendell Holmes *(1809-1894) American author and poet.*

It is a fine thing to have ability, but the ability to discover ability in others is the true test.

Elbert Hubbard *(1856-1915) American editor, publisher, and author of the mora*

Adaptability

- Take the world as it is, not as it ought to be.

  German proverb

- It is a wise person that adapts themselves to all contingencies; it's the fool who always struggles like a swimmer against the current.

  Unknown Source

- They are as much for Mars, as for Mercury; as well qualified for war, as for business.

  Unknown Source

- They that will not apply new remedies must expect new evils.

  Francis Bacon *(1561-1626) British statesman and philosopher.*

- In war as in life, it is often necessary when some cherished scheme has failed, to take up the best alternative open, and if so, it is folly not to work for it with all your might.

  Winston Churchill *(1874-1965) British politician.*

- Adaptability is not imitation. It means power of resistance and assimilation.

  Mahatma Gandhi (1869-1948) *Preeminent leader of Indian nationalism.*

Attitude

- We don't see things as they are, we see things as we are.
  Anaïs Nin *(1903-1977) French author.*
- It's not what happens to you, but how you react to it that matters.
  Epictetus *(50-120) Greek philosopher.*
- We awaken in others the same attitude of mind we hold toward them.
  Elbert Hubbard *(1856-1915) American editor, publisher, and author of the mora*
- The greatest discovery of my generation is that human beings can alter their lives by altering their attitudes of mind.
  William James *(1842-1910) American philosopher and psychologist.*
- It is our attitude at the beginning of a difficult task which, more than anything else, will affect its successful outcome.
  William James *(1842-1910) American philosopher and psychologist.*
- One's destination is never a place, but rather a new way of looking at things.
  Henry Miller *(1891-1980) American author.*
- Nothing can stop the man with the right mental attitude from achieving his goal; nothing on earth can help the man with the wrong mental attitude.
  Thomas Jefferson *(1743-1826) Third president of the United States.*
- A pessimist and an optimist, so much the worse; so much the better.
  Jean de La Fontaine *(1621-1695) French poet.*
- Certain thoughts are prayers. There are moments when, whatever be the attitude of the body, the soul is on its knees.
  Victor Hugo *(1802-1885) French poet, dramatist and novelist.*
- Events will take their course, it is no good of being angry at them; he is happiest who wisely turns them to the best account.
  Euripides *(BC 480-BC 406) Greek tragic poet.*
- Beauty

Everything has beauty, but not everyone sees it.

Confucius *(BC 551-BC 479) Chinese philosopher.*
- The best part of beauty is that which no picture can express.
  Francis Bacon *(1561-1626) British statesman and philosopher.*
- The average girl would rather have beauty than brains because she knows the average man can see much better than he can think.
  Unknown Source
- Beauty is not caused. It is.
  Emily Dickinson *(1830-1886) American poet.*
- To me, fair friend, you never can be old. For as you were when first your eye I eyed. Such seems your beauty still.
  William Shakespeare *(1564-1616) British poet and playwright.*
- It is better to be beautiful than to be good, but it is better to be good than to be ugly.
  Oscar Wilde *(1854-1900) Irish poet and dramatist.*
- Nothing can be beautiful which is not true.
  John Ruskin *(1819-1900) English art critic.*
- Beauty is a primeval phenomenon, which itself never makes its appearance, but the reflection of which is visible in a thousand different utterances of the creative mind, and is as various as nature herself.
  Johann Wolfgang Von Goethe *(1749-1832) German poet, novelist and dramatist.*
- A thing of beauty is a joy for ever: Its loveliness increases; it will never pass into nothingness; but still will keep a bower quiet for us, and a sleep full of sweet dreams, and health, and quiet breathing...
  John Keats *(1795-1821) British poet.*
- Beauty is a harmonious relation between something in our nature and the quality of the object which delights us.
  Blaise Pascal *(1623-1662) French mathematician, physicist and philosopher.*

Character

- Watch your thoughts; they become words. Watch your words; they become actions. Watch your actions; they become habits. Watch your habits; they become character. Watch your character; it becomes your destiny.
  Unknown Source
- Men of genius are admired, men of wealth are envied, men of power are feared; but only men of character are trusted.
  Unknown Source
- One can easily judge the character of a person by the way they treat people who can do nothing for them.
  Proverb
- The measure of a man's real character is what he would do if he knew he would never be found out.
  Thomas B. Macaulay *(1800-1859) English politician, essayist and poet.*
- If you create an act, you create a habit. If you create a habit, you create a character. If you create a character, you create a destiny.
  André Maurois *(1885-1967) French writer.*
- Reputation is what men and women think of us. Character is what God and the angels know of us.
  Thomas Paine *(1737-1809) English intellectual.*
- If you stand straight, do not fear a crooked shadow.
  Chinese proverb
- Clear conscience never fears midnight knocking.
  Chinese proverb
- Character is like a tree and reputation like its shadow. The shadow is what we think of it; the tree is the real thing.
  Abraham Lincoln *(1809-1865) Politician. President of the United States.*
- Show me the man you honor, and I will know what kind of a man you are. It shows me what your ideal of manhood is, and what kind of a man you long to be.
  Thomas Carlyle *(1795-1881) British historian and essayist.*

Charity

- It is more agreeable to have the power to give than to receive.
  Winston Churchill *(1874-1965) British politician.*
- Charity begins at home, but should not end there.
  Thomas Fuller *(1608-1661) British clergyman and author.*
- We ourselves feel that what we are doing is just a drop in the ocean. But if that drop was not in the ocean, I think the ocean would be less because of that missing drop. I do not agree with the big way of doing things.
  Mother Teresa *(1910-1997) Albanian-born missionary.*
- In charity there is no excess.
  Francis Bacon *(1561-1626) British statesman and philosopher.*
- Every charitable act is a stepping stone towards heaven.
  Henry Ward Beecher *(1813-1887) American politician.*
- A man who sees another man on the street corner with only a stump for an arm will be so shocked the first time he'll give him sixpence. But the second time it'll only be a three penny bit. And if he sees him a third time, he'll have him cold-bloodedly handed over to the police.
  Bertolt Brecht *(1898-1956) German writer.*
- Having leveled my palace, don't erect a hovel and complacently admire your own charity in giving me that for a home.
  Emily Bronte *(1818-1848) British novelist and poet.*
- Charity should begin at home, but should not stay there.
  Phillips Brooks *(1835-1893) American Episcopal clergyman.*
- Be charitable before wealth makes you covetous.
  Sir Thomas Browne *(1605-1682) English author.*
- Charity But how shall we expect charity towards others, when we are uncharitable to ourselves? Charity begins at home, is the voice of the world; yet is every man his greatest enemy, and, as it were, his own executioner.
  Sir Thomas Browne *(1605-1682) English author.*

Courage

- It is not because things are difficult that we do not dare; it is because we do not dare that they are difficult.
  Lucius Annaeus Seneca *(4 BC-65) Roman philosopher and playwright.*
- Life becomes real only when we begin to face and solve our own problems. Until then we only swim in circles in a large fantasy world which tends to make us very tired of living. Don't waste energy! Face life now!
  Unknown Source
- Courage is not limited to the battlefield or the Indianapolis 500 or bravely catching a thief in your house. The real tests of courage are much quieter. They are the inner tests, like remaining faithful when nobody's looking, like enduring pain when the room is empty, like standing alone when you're misunderstood.
  Unknown Source
- It's not the size of the dog in the fight, it's the size of the fight in the dog.
  Mark Twain *(1835-1910) U.S. humorist, writer, and lecturer.*
- A person who walks in another's tracks leaves no footprints.
  Unknown Source
- Courage leads to heaven; fear leads to death.
  Lucius Annaeus Seneca *(4 BC-65) Roman philosopher and playwright.*
- Courage is resistance to fear, mastery of fear -- not absence of fear.
  Mark Twain *(1835-1910) U.S. humorist, writer, and lecturer.*
- Courage is the first of human qualities because it is the quality which guarantees all others.
  Winston Churchill *(1874-1965) British politician.*
- The ideas that have lighted my way and, time after time, have given me new courage to face life cheerfully have been Kindness, Beauty, and Truth.
  Albert Einstein *(1879-1955) German-Swiss-U.S. scientist.*
- The ideal man bears the accidents of life with dignity and grace, making the best of circumstances.
  Aristotle *(384 BC-322 BC) Greek philosopher.*

Courtesy

- Life may be not so short but that there is always time for courtesy.
  Ralph Waldo Emerson *(1803-1882) U.S. poet, essayist and lecturer.*
- Life is short, but there is always time for courtesy.
  Ralph Waldo Emerson *(1803-1882) U.S. poet, essayist and lecturer.*
- We must be as courteous to a man as we are to a picture, which we are willing to give the advantage of a good light.
  Ralph Waldo Emerson *(1803-1882) U.S. poet, essayist and lecturer.*
- All doors open to courtesy.
  Thomas Fuller *(1608-1661) British clergyman and author.*
- There is a courtesy of the heart; it is allied to love. From its springs the purest courtesy in the outward behavior.
  Johann Wolfgang Von Goethe *(1749-1832) German poet, novelist and dramatist.*
- It is better to have too much courtesy than too little, provided you are not equally courteous to all, for that would be injustice.
  Baltasar Gracian *(1601-1658) Spanish Philosopher, and Writer.*
- Intelligence and courtesy not always are combined; Often in a wooden house a golden room we find.
  Henry Wadsworth Longfellow *(1807-1882) U.S. poet.*
- True politeness consists in being easy one's self, and in making every one about one as easy as one can.
  Alexander Pope *(1688-1744) English poet and satirist.*
- To speak kindly does not hurt the tongue.
  Proverb
- Men, like bullets, go farthest when they are smoothest.
  Jean Paul *(1763-1825) German novelist and humorist.*

Dignity

- Our dignity is not in what we do, but what we understand.
  George Santayana *(1863-1952) American philosopher and poet.*

- Dignity consists not in possessing honors, but in the consciousness that we deserve them.

  Aristotle *(384 BC-322 BC) Greek philosopher.*
- Every man has his dignity. I'm willing to forget mine, but at my own discretion and not when someone else tells me to.

  Denis Diderot *(1713-1784) French philosopher.*
- Perhaps the only true dignity of man is his capacity to despise himself.

  George Santayana *(1863-1952) American philosopher and poet.*

Generosity

- Generosity lies less in giving much than in giving at the right moment.

  Jean de la Bruyère *(1645-1696) French satiric moralist.*
- Many people are capable of doing a wise thing, more a cunning thing, but very few a generous thing.

  Alexander Pope *(1688-1744) English poet and satirist.*
- What is called generosity is usually only the vanity of giving; we enjoy the vanity more than the thing given.

  François de La Rochefoucauld *(1613-1680) French writer.*
- If you're a generous person you'll have no trouble admitting that somebody else is good. If you're a better person you'll find it's total impossibility.

  Unknown Source
- Liberality consists less in giving a great deal than in gifts well-timed.

  Jean de la Bruyère *(1645-1696) French satiric moralist.*
- Generosity during life is a very different thing from generosity in the hour of death; one proceeds from genuine liberality and benevolence, the other from pride or fear.

  Horace Mann *(1796-1859) U.S. educator.*

- Generosity is nothing else than a craze to possess. All which I abandon, all which I give, I enjoy in a higher manner through the fact that I give it away. To give is to enjoy possessively the object which one gives.

  Jean-Paul Sartre *(1905-1980) French writer and philosopher.*
- The poor don't know that their function in life is to exercise our generosity.

  Jean-Paul Sartre *(1905-1980) French writer and philosopher.*
- Is it not odd that the only generous person I ever knew, who had money to be generous with, should be a stockbroker.

  Percy Bysshe Shelley *(1792-1822) English poet.*
- It is always so pleasant to be generous, though very vexatious to pay debts.

  Ralph Waldo Emerson *(1803-1882) U.S. poet, essayist and lecturer.*

Goodness

- Only happy people can learn. Only happy people can teach. Our religion should put a sparkle in our eyes and a tone in our voice, and a spring in our step that bears witness of our faith and confidence in the goodness of God.

  Unknown Source
- Our will is always for our own good, but we do not always see what that is.

  Jean Jacques Rousseau (1712-1778) *Swiss political philosopher and essayist.*
- Look for no reward in goodness but goodness itself.

  Unknown Source
- Nothing leads to good that is not natural.

  Johann Friedrich Von Schiller (1759-1805) *German dramatist, poet and historian*
- How far that little candle throws its beams! So shines a good dead in a naughty world.

William Shakespeare (1564-1616) British poet and playwright.
- A man, to be greatly good, must imagine intensely and comprehensively; he must put himself in the place of another and of many others; the pains and pleasures of his species must become his own.
Percy Bysshe Shelley (1792-1822) English poet.
- Goodness is the only investment which never fails.
Author.

Grace

- Grace in women has more effect than beauty.
William Hazlitt *(1778-1830) British essayist.*
- Grace is the absence of everything that indicates pain or difficulty, hesitation or incongruity.
William Hazlitt *(1778-1830) British essayist.*
- Grace is in garments, in movements, in manners; beauty in the nude, and in forms. This is true of bodies; but when we speak of feelings, beauty is in their spirituality, and grace in their moderation.
Joseph Joubert *(1754-1824) French moralist.*
- Gracefulness is to the body what understanding is to the mind.
François de La Rochefoucauld *(1613-1680) French writer.*
- Grace is the beauty of form under the influence of freedom.
Johann Friedrich Von Schiller *(1759-1805) German dramatist, poet and historian*
- A graceful and pleasing figure is a perpetual letter of recommendation.
Francis Bacon *(1561-1626) British statesman and philosopher.*
- God appoints our graces to be nurses to other men's weaknesses.
Henry Ward Beecher *(1813-1887) American politician.*
- Grace has been defined as the outward expression of the inward harmony of the soul.
William Hazlitt *(1778-1830) British essayist.*

Honesty

- Look a man in the eye and say what you really think, don't just smile at him and say what you're supposed to think.
  Unknown Source
- Honesty is the best policy. If I lose mine honor, I lose myself.
  William Shakespeare *(1564-1616) British poet and playwright.*
- There is no right way to do something wrong.
  Unknown Source
- I hope I shall possess firmness and virtue enough to maintain what I consider the most enviable of all titles, the character of an honest man.
  George Washington *(1732-1799) First President of the USA.*
- If you follow only one rule, let it be this one: Be yourself. The really strong boy-girl relationships are based on what people really are, not on what they pretend to be.
  Unknown Source
- Honesty is the first chapter of the book of wisdom.
  Thomas Jefferson *(1743-1826) Third president of the United States.*
- Dishonest people conceal their faults from themselves as well as others, honest people know and confess them.
  Christian Nevell Bovee *(1820-1904) American author y lawyer.*
- Be true to your work, your word, and your friend.
  Henry David Thoreau *(1817-1862) American naturalist, poet and philosopher.*
- Honesty is the best policy when there is money in it.
  Mark Twain *(1835-1910) U.S. humorist, writer, and lecturer.*
- Though I am not naturally honest, I am so sometimes by chance.
  William Shakespeare *(1564-1616) British poet and playwright.*

Integrity

- Nothing is at last sacred but the integrity of your own mind.
  Ralph Waldo Emerson *(1803-1882) U.S. poet, essayist and lecturer.*

- A person is not given integrity. It results from the relentless pursuit of honesty at all times.

  Unknown Source
- Integrity without knowledge is weak and useless, and knowledge without integrity is dangerous and dreadful.

  Samuel Johnson *(1709-1784) British author.*
- The person who is slowest in making a promise is most faithful in its performance.

  Jean Jacques Rousseau *(1712-1778) Swiss political philosopher and essayist.*
- A man can do only what a man can do. But if he does that each day he can sleep at night and do it again the next day.

  Albert Schweitzer *(1875-1965) German theologian, philosopher, and physician.*
- In failing circumstances no one can be relied on to keep their integrity.

  Ralph Waldo Emerson *(1803-1882) U.S. poet, essayist and lecturer.*
- The Lord doesn't ask about your ability, only your availability; and, if you prove your dependability, the Lord will increase your capability.

  Unknown Source
- It is far better to be trusted and respected that it is to be liked.

  Unknown Source
- The slow man with integrity will ultimately catch the swift one who has none.

  Unknown Source
- I cannot and will not recant anything, for to go against conscience is neither right nor safe. Here I stand, I can do no other, so help me God. Amen.

  Martin Luther *(1483-1546) German priest and scholar.*

Kindness

- I expect to pass through this world but once. Any good therefore that I can do, or any kindness that I can show to any fellow creature, let me do it now. Let me not defer or neglect it, for I shall not pass this way again.

William Penn (1644-1718) British religious leader.

- Kind words can be short and easy to speak, but their echoes are truly endless.

    Mother Teresa (1910-1997) Albanian-born missionary.

- Let no one ever come to you without leaving better and happier. Be the living expression of God's kindness: kindness in your face, kindness in your eyes, kindness in your smile.

    Mother Teresa (1910-1997) Albanian-born missionary.

- I have wept in the night for the shortness of sight that to somebody's need made me blind; But I never have yet Felt a tinge of regret for being a little to kind

    Unknown Source

- Be kind to unkind people -- they need it the most.

    Unknown Source

- Constant kindness can accomplish much. As the sun makes ice melt, kindness causes misunderstanding, mistrust, and hostility to evaporate.

    Albert Schweitzer (1875-1965) German theologian, philosopher, and physician.

- Kind words are worth much and they cost little.

    Proverb

- Recompense injury with justice, and recompense kindness with kindness.

    Confucius (BC 551-BC 479) Chinese philosopher.

- You cannot do a kindness too soon, for you never know how soon it will be too late.

    Ralph Waldo Emerson (1803-1882) U.S. poet, essayist and lecturer.

- Be the kind of person you would like to be with.

    Unknown Source

Loyalty

- Loyalty means nothing unless it has at its heart the absolute principle of self-sacrifice.
  Woodrow T. Wilson *(1856-1924) Twenty-eighth President of the USA.*
- Had I but served my God with half the zeal I served my King, He would not in mine age have left me naked to mine enemies.
  William Shakespeare *(1564-1616) British poet and playwright.*
- If you are not too long, I will wait here for you all my life.
  Oscar Wilde *(1854-1900) Irish poet and dramatist.*
- Histories are more full of examples of the fidelity of dogs than of friends.
  Alexander Pope *(1688-1744) English poet and satirist.*
- A jack of both sides, is before long, trusted by nobody, and abused by both parties.
  Proverb
  It is better to be faithful than famous.
  Theodore Roosevelt *(1858-1919) 26th president of the U.S.*
- It is difficult to discriminate the voice of truth from amid the clamor raised by heated partisans.
  Johann Friedrich Von Schiller *(1759-1805) German dramatist, poet and historian*
- Fidelity purchased with money, money can destroy.
  Lucius Annaeus Seneca *(4 BC-65) Roman philosopher and playwright.*
  Birds of a feather flock together.
  Proverb
- Total loyalty is possible only when fidelity is emptied of all concrete content, from which changes of mind might naturally arise.
  Hannah Arendt *(1906-1975) German-born American political philosopher.*

Self-control

- Self-disciplined begins with the mastery of your thoughts. If you don't control what you think, you can't control what you do.

Simply, self-discipline enables you to think first and act afterward.
- Hill, Napoleon

Napoleon Hill *(1883-1970) American speaker and motivational writer.*

- He who conquers himself is the mightiest warrior.

  Confucius *(BC 551-BC 479) Chinese philosopher.*

- I count him braver who overcomes his desires than him who conquers his enemies; for the hardest victory is over self.

  Aristotle *(384 BC-322 BC) Greek philosopher.*

- The highest possible stage in moral culture is when we recognize that we ought to control our thoughts.

  Charles Darwin *(1809-1882) English Naturalist*

- Why are we so full of restraint? Why do we not give in all directions? Is it fear of losing ourselves? Until we do lose ourselves there is no hope of finding ourselves.

  Henry Miller *(1891-1980) American author.*

- He who cannot obey himself will be commanded. That is the nature of living creatures.

  Friedrich Nietzsche *(1844-1900) German-Swiss philosopher and writer.*

- O, it is excellent to have a giant's strength, but it is tyrannous to use it like a giant.

  William Shakespeare *(1564-1616) British poet and playwright.*

- I am always with myself and it is I who am my tormentor. - Tolstoy, Count Leo

  Leo Tolstoy *(1828-1910) Russian writer.*

- Govern thyself then you will be able to govern the world.

  Unknown Source

- To enjoy freedom we have to control ourselves.

  Virginia Woolf *(1882-1941) British novelist and essayist.*

Sympathy

- Strengthen me by sympathizing with my strength, not my weakness.

  Amos Bronson Alcott *(1799-1888) American educator.*

- Sympathy is a supporting atmosphere, and in it we unfold easily and well.

  Ralph Waldo Emerson *(1803-1882) U.S. poet, essayist and lecturer.*
- No man needs sympathy because he has to work. Far and away the best prize that life offers is the chance to work hard at work worth doing.

  Theodore Roosevelt *(1858-1919) 26th president of the U.S.*
- We pity in others only the those evils which we ourselves have experienced.

  Jean Jacques Rousseau *(1712-1778) Swiss political philosopher and essayist.*
- There is nothing sweeter than to be sympathized with.

  George Santayana *(1863-1952) American philosopher and poet.*
- The capacity to give one's attention to a sufferer is a very rare and difficult thing; it is almost a miracle; it is a miracle. Nearly all those who think they have this capacity do not possess it. Warmth of heart, impulsiveness, pity are not enough.

  Simone Weil *(1910-1943) French Philosopher*
- And whoever walks a furlong without sympathy walks to his own funeral drest in his shroud.

  Walt Whitman *(1819-1892) American poet.*
- Sympathy with joy intensifies the sum of sympathy in the world, sympathy with pain does not really diminish the amount of pain.

  Oscar Wilde *(1854-1900) Irish poet and dramatist.*
- There is something terribly morbid in the modern sympathy with pain. One should sympathize with the color, the beauty, the joy of life. The less said about life's sores the better.

  Oscar Wilde *(1854-1900) Irish poet and dramatist.*
- Seldom in the business and transactions of ordinary life, do we find the sympathy we want.

  Johann Wolfgang Von Goethe *(1749-1832) German poet, novelist and dramatist.*

Tolerance

- As no roads are so rough as those that have just been mended, so no sinners are so intolerant as those that have just turned saints.
  Charles Caleb Colton *(1780-1832) British clergyman, sportsman and author.*
- Tolerance is only another name for indifference.
  W. Somerset Maugham *(1874-1965) British novelist and playwright.*
- Whenever you hold a fellow creature in distress, remember that he is a man.
  Lucius Annaeus Seneca *(4 BC-65) Roman philosopher and playwright.*
- When tolerance is not afforded to those so well-deserved, it speaks ill of the one who feels he cannot afford to give it.
  Unknown Source
- Intolerance betrays want of faith in one's cause.
  Mahatma Gandhi *(1869-1948) Pre-eminent leader of Indian nationalism.*
- Toleration is good for all, or it is good for none.
  Edmund Burke *(1729-1797) British political writer.*
- There is a limit at which forbearance ceases to be a virtue.
  Edmund Burke *(1729-1797) British political writer.*
- I have seen great intolerance shown in support of tolerance.
  Samuel Taylor Coleridge *(1772-1834) British poet, critic, and philosopher*

Thoughts

"A man's life is what his thoughts make him." (Marcus Aurelius)

Trials

"When God wants to make a man, he puts him into some storm." (Lettie Cowman)
"Adversity is the dust Heaven polishes its jewels with." (Unknown)

"When life becomes all snarled up, offer it to our Lord and let Him untie the knots." (Book of Days for Christians)

"Outward losses drive good people to their prayers but bad people to their curses." (Henry)

"It is said that in some countries trees will grow, but will bear no fruit because there is no winter there." (John Bunyan)

Truth

"No matter what the postmodern world concludes about God and truth, reality is that God is still God, and He is still trying to reconcile men unto Himself." (Dr. Sam Horn)

"Truth is incontrovertible. Panic may resent it; ignorance may deride it; malice may distort it; but there it is." (Winston Churchill)

"It is truth that passes into action that produces righteousness." (Richard Bennett)

"To hear the truth and not accept it does not nullify truth." (Brotherhood Journal)

"Truth is not ultimately a matter of pride or humility, it is a matter of fact." (Unknown)

"Always tell the truth. Then you don't have to worry about what you said last." (Robert Cook)

"Your teeth may be false, but always let your tongue be true." [unknown]

"Beware of a half truth; you may bet hold of the wrong half." [unknown]

"Truth fears nothing but concealment." [unknown}

Unbelief

"Unbelief is the mother of vice; it is the parent of sin; and, therefore, I say it is a pestilent evil-a master sin." [Charles H. Spurgeon]

Values

"For what shall it profit a man, if he shall gain the whole world, and lose his own soul? Or what shall a man give in exchange for his souls?" (Mark 8:36, 37)

"People who have no values have no value."   (Burton Hills)
"He is no fool who gives up that which he cannot keep to gain that which he cannot lose." (Jim Elliot)

Virtue

"Virtue is the doing of good to mankind in the obedience tot he will of God, and for the sake of everlasting happiness." [William Paley]
"Virtue is to the soul what health is tot he body." [Francios de La Rochefoucauld]

Vision

"Vision must be followed by venture. It is not enough to stare at the steps - we must step up the stairs." (Vance Havner)

Wealth

"No man can serve two masters: for either he will hate the one, and love the other; or else he will hold to the one, and despise the other. Ye cannot serve God and mammon." (Jesus in Matthew 6:24)
"The poorest man is he whose only wealth is money." (unknown)

Will of God

"You can't do the will of God if you don't know the Word of God." [Jack Wyrtzen]

Wisdom

"Wisdom is, and starts with, the humility to accept the fact that you don't have all the right answers, and the courage to learn to ask the right questions." [Anonymous]

Worship

"It is only when men begin to worship that they begin to grow." (Coolidge)

"One thing have I desired of the LORD, that will I seek after; that I may dwell in the house of the LORD all the days of my life, to behold the beauty of the LORD, and to enquire in his temple." (Psalm 27:4)

"Religious externals may have meaning for the God-inhabited soul; for any others they are not only useless but may actually become snares, deceiving them into a false and perilous sense of security." (A. W. Tozer)